# Praise for *Desired by God*

"Love! I don't get it. Neither do you. It is indescribable. It is incomprehensible. But, it can be given and accepted. It's not an emotion. You know when someone loves you and when you love someone. My friend Van Moody unpacks all of that in *Desired by God*. For God so loved . . . and loves—you!"

—SAM CHAND, LEADERSHIP CONSULTANT, AUTHOR OF *LEADERSHIP PAIN*

"If you have a fire in your heart for Jesus, this book is pure gasoline. It brushes away the wet leaves of religion and breathes passion back into your intimate spiritual life. This one is truly unique and I highly recommend it."

—DR. JONATHAN WELTON, BESTSELLING AUTHOR,
PRESIDENT OF WELTON ACADEMY

"*Desired by God* is a game changer. . . . A must-read. But more importantly it is a guide to the romanticism of a God who has chosen us to be the object of His affection!"

—BISHOP T. D. JAKES SR., SENIOR PASTOR,
THE POTTER'S HOUSE OF DALLAS

"No matter whether you're a new believer or a follower of Jesus for decades, this book will startle you with the powerful love of God in ways you've never considered. Highly recommended!"

—CHRIS HODGES, SENIOR PASTOR, CHURCH OF THE
HIGHLANDS; AUTHOR OF *THE DANIEL DILEMMA*

"Van Moody gives us unusual insight into the power, the practicality, and the purposeful presence of the love of the God who does not love—but who *is* love.

—KENNETH C. ULMER, DMIN, PHD,
COCHAIRMAN, THE KING'S UNIVERSITY

"*Desired by God* arrestingly reveals the power of a living, loving relationship with God . . . a much-needed text making a real contribution to scholarship and practical theology."

—Cynthia Rembert James, PhD, DMin,
associate pastor, The Potters House of Dallas

"Life-affirming lessons to ease your journey and inspire your purpose, *Desired by God* is an on-time treasure from a relevant leader of the times."

—Nicole LaBeach, PhD, Volition Enterprises

"With the skill of an able teacher, and the compassion of a faithful pastor, Van Moody guides us on a journey into God's love so we can accept it for ourselves and then offer it to our broken and love-starved world."

—Stephen Chapin Garner, DMin, senior minister,
The Congregational Church of New Canaan

"Van Moody does an excellent job of showing us who God is, stripped of the facades and myths of religious understanding—a loving Father who has always been good. Prepare yourself to love and be loved in ways that almost seem too good to be true!"

—Matthew Hester, ThD, author; pastor,
Dominion Church International

"Anyone who needs to know that they are God's number one priority or for those of us who every now and then need to be reassured of God's great unfailing love for us should purchase two copies of *Desired by God*. One for yourself and the other for a friend, coworker, or stranger."

—Carolyn Ann Knight, DMin,
seminary advisor and professor of homiletics

"Van Moody's new book will cause you to be overwhelmed by God's unfathomable love for you! It will deepen your understanding and draw you closer to God like a magnet draws steel."

—Bishop Dale C. Bronner, DMin, founder and senior pastor,
Word of Faith Family Worship Cathedral

"*Desired by God* thrusts you to comprehend God's desire for you, it transforms your current knowledge of salvation, and it unpacks why HE revealed Himself, and why HE died for us. It's a must-read."

—Bishop Eric D. Garnes, DMin, MPS Presiding Prelate,
United Covenant Churches of Christ;
senior pastor, Tabernacle of Praise Cathedral

"You will walk away with a new understanding of *real* love and your life will truly be impacted after reading this book."

—Pastor John K. Jenkins Sr., senior pastor,
First Baptist Church of Glenarden

"*Desired by God* taps into the depth of the immeasurable love God has for us and His desire to foster a richer, more expansive, level of intimacy with all people. I'm certain that this insightful must-read will be a welcomed addition to your library."

—Bishop Kenneth H. Dupree, senior pastor, The Victory Church

"With so many people and things competing for our attention, *Desired by God* brings us back to the core of who we are and why we exist. Be prepared for your love life to absolutely be revolutionized and let your commitment to pursue God grow with each chapter!"

—Jamal Bryant, DMin, senior pastor, Empowerment Temple

"*Desired by God* will enable you to experience the love of God in a fresh new way, which will nurture more peace, joy, fulfillment, and transformation in your life."

—Lonnie J. Oliver, DMin, pastor emeritus,
New Life Presbyterian Church

"Van Moody clearly underscores that when we accept the love God gives to us, we make ourselves available to the deep treasures that come from a God who is an unending source of goodness, grace, and mercy."

—Craig L. Oliver, Sr., DMin, senior pastor,
Elizabeth Baptist Church

"Van Moody brings his unique spiritual insight to the most crucial relationship of all—your relationship with God. Well written, inspirational, and life changing. Read, explore, and be transformed!"

—LEVY H. KNOX, BISHOP AND FOUNDER, LIVING WORD
CHRISTIAN CENTER INTERNATIONAL MINISTRIES; KINGDOM
NETWORK OF CHURCHES INTERNATIONAL (KNCI);
OPPORTUNITY FOR UNITY MINISTRY NETWORK (OFU)

"A chapter by chapter window into the heart of our Creator. The God who made us is the same God who is passionately in love with us and personally pursues us. Read this book!"

—ALBERT TATE, LEAD PASTOR, FELLOWSHIP MONROVIA

"Van Moody has taken a concept as abstract as divine love and crafted a foundation concrete enough for a lifelong faith to be built upon it."

—WAYNE CHANEY JR., AUTHOR; TV PERSONALITY;
SENIOR PASTOR, ANTIOCH CHURCH, LONG BEACH

"In a seemingly love-starved generation, Moody brilliantly infuses fresh life into the timeless and unwavering presence of God's love. He brokers and mirrors through prose the supernatural movement of reconciliation between God and his beloved, mankind."

—MYESHA CHANEY, AUTHOR; TV PERSONALITY; FOUNDER,
HIDING BEHIND THE LIPSTICK MOVEMENT

"A compelling, thought-provoking, and life-altering masterpiece. As you comb through the pages and allow the words to reverberate throughout the core of your being, I promise your life will be transformed."

—DEMETRIUS MILES, FOUNDING AND SENIOR PASTOR,
TUCSON CHURCH INTERNATIONAL, TUCSON, ARIZONA

"With intellectual acuity and the passion of a shepherd, Van Moody navigates us straight into the heart of God. This book must be taken seriously."

—JODY MOORE, SENIOR PASTOR, PRAISE TABERNACLE BIBLE CHURCH

"A powerful description and a passionate invitation to participate in a loving relationship with almighty God. . . . Another must-read!"

—Jerry L. Cannon DMin, senior pastor,
C.N. Jenkins Memorial Presbyterian Church

"In *Desired by God*, we learn why loving God is not only the greatest commandment but it is truly the reciprocity of the greatest love affair we will ever know. What an eye-opening demonstration of the power of true unyielding love."

—Art Franklin, TV news anchor

"Ours is a meritocracy which says a person's worth is constructed on the scaffolding of their performance. But God has come to do violence to the meritocracy by emancipating us from such performance nonsense. . . . When you're finished reading you will exhale, and thank God that like Jesus you, too, are His beloved son, His beloved daughter, in whom He is well pleased."

—Bryan Loritts, lead pastor, Abundant Life; author

"Through the use of stories and biographical realities each of us is empowered to develop a fresh revelation of the all-encompassing Love of God."

—Bishop Kim Brown, senior pastor, The Mount

"Van Moody puts the spotlight on the most important relationship of all—the one we share with our Creator. After reading this book, you will walk away understanding the power of true love . . . in awe of the passionate, everlasting love God has for you.

—De'Andre Salter, lead pastor of Impact Church

"This book redefines the meaning, purpose, and real power of love through God's desire for and relationship with each of us."

—Lisa Herring, EdD, Superintendent, Birmingham City Schools

"Van's ability to communicate God's heart and love for you with accuracy and clarity is refreshing as well as liberating. I encourage all who desire to walk in God's plan and purpose to pick up this book and devour it cover to cover. You won't regret it."

—MARTIJN VAN TILBORGH, SPEAKER, AUTHOR, AND ENTREPRENEUR

# DESIRED BY GOD

Discover a Strong, Soul-Satisfying Relationship with God by
Understanding Who He Is and How Much He Loves You

## Van Moody

With Susy Flory

NELSON
BOOKS

An Imprint of Thomas Nelson

Published in Nashville, Tennessee, by Nelson Books, an imprint of Thomas Nelson. Nelson Books and Thomas Nelson are registered trademarks of HarperCollins Christian Publishing, Inc.

Thomas Nelson titles may be purchased in bulk for educational, business, fund-raising, or sales promotional use. For information, please e-mail SpecialMarkets@ThomasNelson.com.

Any Internet addresses, phone numbers, or company or product information printed in this book are offered as a resource and are not intended in any way to be or to imply an endorsement by Thomas Nelson, nor does Thomas Nelson vouch for the existence, content, or services of these sites, phone numbers, companies, or products beyond the life of this book.

Unless otherwise noted, Scripture quotations are taken from the Holy Bible, New International Version®, NIV®. Copyright © 1973, 1978, 1984, 2011 by Biblica, Inc.® Used by permission of Zondervan. All rights reserved worldwide. www.Zondervan.com. The "NIV" and "New International Version" are trademarks registered in the United States Patent and Trademark Office by Biblica, Inc.® Scripture quotations marked AMPC are from the Amplified® Bible, Classic Edition, copyright © 1954, 1958, 1962, 1964, 1965, 1987 by The Lockman Foundation. Used by permission. (www.Lockman.org) Scripture quotations marked CEV are from the Contemporary English Version. Copyright © 1991, 1992, 1995 by American Bible Society. Used by permission. Scripture quotations marked ESV are from the ESV® Bible (The Holy Bible, English Standard Version®). Copyright © 2001 by Crossway, a publishing ministry of Good News Publishers. Used by permission. All rights reserved. Scripture quotations marked THE MESSAGE are from The Message. Copyright © by Eugene H. Peterson 1993, 1994, 1995, 1996, 2000, 2001, 2002. Used by permission of NavPress. All rights reserved. Represented by Tyndale House Publishers, Inc. Scripture quotations marked NASB are from New American Standard Bible®. Copyright © 1960, 1962, 1963, 1968, 1971, 1972, 1973, 1975, 1977, 1995 by The Lockman Foundation. Used by permission. (www.Lockman.org) Scripture quotations marked NLT are from the Holy Bible, New Living Translation. © 1996, 2004, 2007, 2013, 2015 by Tyndale House Foundation. Used by permission of Tyndale House Publishers, Inc., Carol Stream, Illinois 60188. All rights reserved. Scripture quotations marked TLB are from The Living Bible. Copyright © 1971. Used by permission of Tyndale House Publishers, Inc., Carol Stream, Illinois 60188. All rights reserved. Scripture quotations marked NKJV are taken from the New King James Version®. © 1982 by Thomas Nelson. Used by permission. All rights reserved. Scriptures marked ISV are from International Standard Version, copyright 1996-2012, ISV Foundation of California, used by permission of Davidson Press, LLC. All rights reserved internationally.

ISBN 978-0-7180-7759-4 (eBook)

**Library of Congress Cataloging-in-Publication Data**

Names: Moody, Van, 1975- author.
Title: Desired by God : discover a strong, soul-satisfying relationship with
    God by understanding who He is and how much He loves you / Van Moody, with
    Susy Flory.
Description: Nashville : Thomas Nelson, 2018. | Includes bibliographical
    references.
Identifiers: LCCN 2017059160 | ISBN 9780718077570
Subjects: LCSH: God (Christianity)--Love. | Kierkegaard, S?ren, 1813-1855.
Classification: LCC BT140 .M67 2018 | DDC 231/.6--dc23 LC record available at https://lccn.loc.
gov/2017059160

*Printed in the United States of America*

18  19  20  21  22    LSC    10  9  8  7  6  5  4  3  2  1

*To everyone looking, longing, or living for God . . .*

*And may you have the power to understand, as all God's people should, how wide, how long, how high, and how deep his love is. May you experience the love of Christ, though it is too great to understand fully. Then you will be made complete with all the fullness of life and power that comes from God."*

—PAUL (EPHESIANS 3:18–19 NLT)

# Contents

## Section 3: Living Loved

# PROLOGUE

# A Love Story

*Love is all, it gives all, and it takes all.*
—Søren Kierkegaard

Once upon a time a young man fell in love with a young woman. To him, she was the most beautiful, intelligent, and wonderful person he'd ever met. She looked like an exquisite blossom from the garden. She smelled like a fresh spring rain. Her voice sounded like the tinkling bells of a fine music box. And he could not stop thinking about her.

*What is she doing right now?* he wondered every waking moment of every single day.

*What is she thinking?*

*Who is she with?*

*Does she miss me as much as I miss her?*

*Does she love me as much as I love her?*

*I wonder if, right now, she might just be thinking of me.*

The man liked to write, and since he was more comfortable putting his feelings down on paper than speaking them out loud, he began to write her letters to pour out his feelings.

"I am only yours," he wrote. "Eternally yours."

In another letter he tried to describe his unquenchable feelings: "In the stillness of midnight, for the day does begin at midnight, and at midnight I awoke and the hours grew long for me, for what is as swift as love? Love is the swiftest of all, swifter than itself."[1] He felt his love growing quickly, and the thought frightened him. He wasn't sure he knew what love was, or how to love a woman the way she deserved to be loved.

The man was the youngest of seven children born into a strict house with a melancholy father who was stern and religious. With so little joy and lightness in the house, he felt like he'd been "born old." As a child, and later as an adolescent, he liked school, loved to learn, and enjoyed his studies, although he wasn't part of the popular crowd. Instead, he tried to impress others with his wit.

As a university student he made mistakes and ended up with some debts, which his father paid. When he finally buckled down to concentrate on his studies, he decided to become a pastor. The opportunity to spend much of his time in intensive study, along with the steady nature of the job, appealed to him. But when he was about to enter seminary, the most beautiful girl he'd ever seen came into his life and changed everything.

The young woman became fond of him, too, and they spent some time together. As their love grew, so did his spirits. "In all of this I am happy, indescribably happy, for I know what I possess. And when it storms and roars in the workshop of my thoughts, I listen for your voice," he wrote.

As their relationship continued, he found he could no longer contain his feelings. He was deeply in love and wanted to be with her every moment of every day. In one of his letters he wrote down his most fervent, passionate wish: "That neither Death, nor Life, nor Angels, nor Principalities, nor Powers, nor the present, nor that which is to come, nor the Exalted, nor the Profound, nor any other creature may tear me from you, or you from me." He was a man in love, and it consumed him from the moment he woke to the moment he closed his eyes at night. His life revolved around her and he thought of nothing else.

The lovestruck man was Søren Kierkegaard, a famous Danish philosopher, and the woman he loved with all his heart was named Regine Olsen. Their love story is a famous one, and Søren put down many of his feelings in his letters both to her and to a close friend.

Have you ever experienced a feeling of love like Søren's? Where your whole life revolved around another person and your feelings for him or her? Love is the most powerful and consuming emotion on the planet, and the feeling can be so strong that you feel overwhelmed with the intensity of it. You are overcome with the desire to love and be loved.

To be lovestruck means to be passionately consumed with someone or something, impacting your life. Your thoughts, emotions, and actions are locked on the object of your love. You can feel this not only for a romantic partner but also for your children, your pets, and even sometimes a pastor, politician, athlete, or entertainer.

Sometimes, the feeling of being in love is intensified when that love is *not* returned. Think about the political hangover and heartache many people feel after a major election when it becomes very difficult for them to understand why other people aren't in love with their candidates or their particular visions of America.

One of my favorite poems about that feeling is "I Wrote a Good Omelet," by Nikki Giovanni. It talks about falling in love and feeling upside down and topsy-turvy, with the poet describing how she can't even tell the different between a poem and an omelet anymore. Have you ever felt that way? Your mind and heart are with someone else, your emotions and thoughts invested in a relationship where your feelings may or may not be completely reciprocated.

It doesn't matter if you're single or married; if you have been around for any period of time, and in any sort of relationship, you know what it feels like to be unabashedly in love. It can be beautiful and wonderful and earthshaking, but it can also be difficult and uncomfortable if the two of you are not in the same exact emotional place. It can be heart wrenching if you are the one who is more deeply and emotionally invested. You're yearning for the love of another and it can hurt.

Yet this is how God made us. God Himself desires to love and be loved. We're created in His image, so it's in our DNA to desire to love and be loved. We have the same yearnings for connection with another being that He has, and the same potential for love that He does.

In the book of Ezekiel, God describes His love for the people of Israel in chapter 16 as if He were talking about a young woman. He freely lavishes her with gifts to enhance her beauty and show His love: "I clothed you with an embroidered dress and put sandals of fine leather on you. I dressed you in fine linen and covered you with costly garments. I adorned you with jewelry: I put bracelets on your arms and a necklace around your neck, and I put a ring on your nose, earrings on your ears and a beautiful crown on your head."

As a lover, God paints a word picture of a woman given the

best of the best to set her apart as special and adored. "So you were adorned with gold and silver; your clothes were of fine linen and costly fabric and embroidered cloth. Your food was honey, olive oil and the finest flour. You became very beautiful and rose to be a queen. And your fame spread among the nations on account of your beauty, because the splendor I had given you made your beauty perfect," said God (vv. 10–14).

After these passionate descriptions of the woman He loves, God declares His love for her with a wedding vow: "I gave you my solemn oath and entered into a covenant with you, declares the Sovereign LORD, and you became mine" (v. 8). He loves her so much He wants her to be His, forever. It's as if He were signing a letter exactly the way Søren did: "I am only yours . . . eternally yours."

In the Old Testament love poem called Song of Songs, God again takes on the persona of a man in love. First, the woman hears a knock: "I slept but my heart was awake. Listen! My beloved is knocking."

"Open to me, my sister, my darling, my dove, my flawless one," He says through the door (5:2). That man at the door is God, calling and knocking on the door of your life because He yearns for a relationship with you.

Just as Søren was in love with Regine, pouring out his heart on the page in pen and ink, so God was in love with His people, lavishing them with the best of everything He had to offer. And He still *is* in love with His people, every one of them, including you. Isn't it wonderful?

You are always in His mind and He wants nothing to come between you and Him. Ever. You are loved and desired by God, every day, every minute. Stop and think about that for a moment.

Not only are you known by God, but you are desired by God. He loves you and He wants you close.

Sometimes we forget about that, as you'll see in the pages ahead. It's important to understand how, even though God loves and relentlessly pursues His people, we often get distracted by life's ups and downs and forget who loves us most. It happened early in human history, and it still happens today. This book is a look at the passionate nature of the God who loves us and explores what it means to understand and embrace that love.

We'll also try to make sense of what it means to live in light of that love, with a deep sense of knowing how much God desires us and wants us to return that desire. Unlike the sometimes complicated love affairs of men and women, God never loses control of Himself while pursuing His beloved, but He will go to the utmost lengths, even the cross, for those He loves. There is no other love story quite like this one.

# INTRODUCTION

# The Love Story to End All Love Stories

*Love recognizes no barriers. It jumps hurdles, leaps fences, penetrates walls to arrive at its destination full of hope.*
—MAYA ANGELOU

Steve Jobs was a man in love. But unlike Kierkegaard, his intense and passionate and all-consuming love was not focused on a particular person. Instead, it was focused on a product. First it was a desktop computer. Next a music-storing and -playing device. Then, finally, a phone.

Steve Jobs loved creating sleek, beautiful, and innovative pieces of technology for our desktops and pockets. People loved him. But why? He's not a hero in the conventional sense—he never led a country or fought a war or defended the innocent. His inventions didn't directly advance the cause of science, save people's lives, or even lengthen them the way medical innovations can. He didn't explore earth, sea, or space, and add to the body of knowledge about the universe. He never even graduated from college. And apparently, he wasn't even a particularly nice person; some family members, friends, and employees have stories to tell about how his love for his products often took precedence over his love for those closest to him. By all accounts, Jobs sometimes chose work over love and products over people.

But each little machine he had a hand in creating was a wonder, its design and functionality springing from a man who seemed obsessed with putting an Apple device or two into the home of almost every American. He changed the way we communicate, gather, and disseminate information. There's an Apple store in almost every big city, and people still gather for new product launches, camping out on the street for the chance to purchase the latest Apple product.

Steve Jobs passed away in 2011, but he's still alive through his products, and the legend of his life and work continues to grow. Yes, he had talent and creativity to spare, but what powered his life and work and innovation was the universe's most powerful emotion: love . . . for his creations.

Jobs said you must truly love what you do for a living. "If you haven't found it yet, keep looking. Don't settle. As with all matters of the heart, you'll know when you find it. And, like any great relationship, it just gets better and better as the years roll on."[1]

The visionary creator also believed you have to pour all your energy, strength, and will into your work. He couldn't rest if his products weren't exactly like what he envisioned: "For you to sleep well at night," Jobs once said, "the aesthetic, the quality, has to be carried all the way through."[2] There were no shortcuts for him, and the intensity of his vision powered the company to success as one of the most valuable brands in the world. In 2015, Apple shattered business records and became the first company with a market value of more than $700 billion.

Steve Jobs's products were like his children, and he wanted them to succeed. His first real success, the innovative Apple Macintosh desktop computer, was precious to him. He called it "the neatest experience of my life . . . none of us wanted to release it at the end. It was as though we knew that once it was out of our hands, it wouldn't be ours anymore."[3] Doesn't that sound like a mother or father, or even a grandparent, talking about a much-loved child?

But human beings fall in love with much more than just other humans or, like Steve, innovative technology. People also fall in love with vibrant cities, beautiful places like beaches or mountain lakes, and even entire countries. Do you know anyone who loves all things French? There's a word in the dictionary for someone who loves France: *Francophile*. It means a person who has a strong affinity toward the French language, French history, French culture, or French people. A Francophile is in love with an entire country and the way they do life.

But for most of us, the love we feel for material things doesn't last because our love is not returned. There's no reciprocal relationship. For love to last, it has to be returned; there needs to be a mutual connection. In the end, France is a country that doesn't really care much about you as a person. And one of these days your Apple product will break and stop working or become obsolete. But the love represented by a relationship with another individual can last, even for eternity.

A well-known woman from India nicknamed Amma

understands the need we have for a close relationship with another person. Amma, or "Mother," is a Hindu spiritual leader who travels the world in a personal mission to show love to as many people as she can.

Amma's real name is Mata Amritanandamayi and she is sixty-three years old. When she was younger, people were drawn to her for comfort and care, and she began to spontaneously embrace people. Now, decades later, people travel across the world and line up for days in order to meet her and receive a loving smile and a hug.

More than thirty-four million people have been hugged by Amma, and she has been known to give out hugs for more than twenty-two hours at a time. She exhibits compassion, tenderness, patience, and solace for those seeking care and spiritual guidance. She will never be as famous or as rich as a Steve Jobs, but she understands much more about love and connection than many other contemporary leaders. Amma gives freely of her attention and her care, and for those precious few minutes in her presence, people report feeling connected, individually loved, and cared for. Receiving a hug from Amma is a revolutionary experience that reportedly changes people's lives. From the outside looking in, it appears that Amma lives a life based on love.

Yet, in the end, as wonderful as Amma seems to be, she is just another human being who has the same struggles and problems that we all do. And I'm guessing she has moments of her own when she doesn't feel particularly loving toward others. That's normal. That's human. I'm also guessing she has moments when *she* doesn't feel loved. That's normal too.

No matter how many family members and friends you have around you, there are times when it feels as if no one else really loves or understands or cares about your problems. Just as products or places eventually lose their luster, with your feelings for them fading away, so it is with human relationships. The feelings ebb and flow over time, and no one loves or feels loved 100 percent of the time. We're all only human, after all. When it comes to loving someone else, we stumble and forget, or mess up and sometimes hurt the other person. We try and try again, but we fail and fail again too.

It's one thing when we're the ones messing up and doing the failing. We feel bad. But we feel even worse when *we* are the ones who are experiencing the results of the failure or shortcoming of a love relationship. It's an unforgettable feeling when we're the ones who are unloved, unwanted, or uncared for. Rejection is the worst feeling in the world, and every single human alive on the planet knows that feeling. You can't live too many years without feeling the sting of rejection or the pain of being unloved. People were made to live in community and with connection, and when that doesn't happen, it's miserable. A hug from Amma is a moment of love and connection, but it's not going to last. We need to feel loved and connected every moment and every day.

In my first book, *The People Factor,* I wrote about how I've listened to thousands of people share a variety of problems and ask for answers and advice. Almost always, those problems stem from relational challenges. After listening to people talk about their problems over the years, I came to understand that relationships are the most important area of our lives. They make us or break us. Relationships with others can be our source of greatest joy or greatest pain. If there is anything more painful than physical illness or injury, it's the emotional ache of a human heart in the throes of rejection.

Every relationship you are a part of influences your life. There are no neutral relationships. Each one lifts you up or weighs you down. It moves you forward or holds you back. It helps you or it hurts you. For a good and happy life, you have to get your relationships right. There are three crucial categories of relationship you must get in order to live your best possible life: your relationships with others, your relationship with yourself, and your relationship with God.

I wrote about the first two categories of relationships in *The People Factor* and in my subsequent book, *The I-Factor.* Those two books, and now this one, are rooted in the story in the gospel of Matthew of Jesus' encounter with a group of smart, highly educated religious leaders. The Pharisees were upset by Jesus' revolutionary teaching, so they continually asked Him questions, trying to trap Him into saying something that would allow them to have Him arrested and silenced. On this occasion, they asked Him which of the hundreds of Jewish laws was *the* most important. Unafraid of the loaded question, Jesus answered, "Love the Lord your God with all your heart and with all your soul and with all your mind. This is the first and greatest commandment."

Jesus didn't stop there but went on to designate the second greatest commandment. "Love your neighbor as yourself. All the Law and the Prophets hang on these two commandments."[4]

Loving God and loving people—Jesus put these two simple principles at the heart of what God's laws are all about. "Love your neighbor as yourself" means that to have a happy life you need to get your relationships with other people, *and* with yourself, right. That is what my first two books are about.

But the book in your hands is about the third—and the most crucial—relationship of all: your relationship with God. Loving the Lord your God with all your heart and with all your soul and with all your mind is important because a healthy, strong, passionate relationship with God is the only way you will feel whole and complete and loved and cared for. That feeling, and the relationship underpinning that feeling, is going to last for a lifetime. In fact, that love relationship with God is going to last for an eternity because God loves you more than Steve Jobs loved his products, more than a Francophile loves France, more than Amma loves giving hugs, and more than Søren loved Regine.

God loves you, and that love lasts and perseveres even though the love of His people toward Him often does not. God is all too familiar with a nonreciprocal cycle of love involving His people. Throughout the Bible, and lasting into His relationships with people today, over and over God's pure and earnest love for people has been given, rejected by the objects of that love, and finally accepted.

## THE CYCLE OF LOVE

### LOVE IS GIVEN—LOVE IS REJECTED—LOVE IS ACCEPTED

In Song of Songs chapter 5, a lover (standing in for God) stands at the door of his beloved and knocks. The woman (who represents each one of us) is already in bed for the night and does not want to get up. When she hears the knock, she responds with, "I have taken off my robe—must I put it on again? I have washed my feet—must I soil them again?" (v. 3). She delays getting up, making excuses for why she won't open the door. Then, by the time she does open the door, he is gone. It's a clear picture of God extending His love to us, pursuing us, and being rejected. Song of Songs is a love poem about God wanting to lavish His love on His people. Not only is this Old Testament book a picture of God's love, but the entire Bible is God's love letter to us.

The reason God desires us is simple: He *is* love, so He gives us love. It's who He is. But the reasons God's love is often rejected are more complicated, and that's what this book is all about. God has created us in His image, so every time we fall in love, whether it's with a book or a band or a sports team or a person, unwittingly we're starting on this same cycle of love. Whether we realize it or not, we're wired the same way as God with the desire to love and be loved. We have the same yearnings for connection through relationships that God does, and sometimes we experience the same love given-rejected-accepted cycle when our relationships don't work out the way we hope.

So who is this God who—as we will discover—loves us even more than a man or woman yearning for his or her lover? To understand God's desire for us, we need a fresh, new, and accurate picture of God. Because before you can connect to God, you have to know Him as He really is. But the problem is that we don't really know or understand God. If we develop or adopt a false picture of who He is, we end up with several problems in our search for a real, authentic relationship with Him:

- Little or no desire for a relationship with Him
- Wrong motivations on our part
- Searching for understanding or knowledge instead of a real relationship

My desire is to give you a fresh and true picture of God as a potential lover—desiring with all His heart for you to know who He really is—so that you will fall in love with Him and return the powerful feelings of love He has for you. When you understand the height and depth and breadth of His love for you, then you can return that love and move forward into a fresh, new life, with new perspective. And when you understand that He loves you in spite of your rejection of Him, well, you're on your way to grasping a little bit more about the nature of God's love for you.

Remember the television show *Cops*, where a TV crew followed police officers around as they carried out their duties? I will never forget one particular episode. An elderly lady in a trailer park had a troubled son whose life had been ruined by drug addiction. He was not in good health, he was missing one of his legs, and he lived with and depended on his mother for help. When the police came to arrest him for something he'd done, the cameras followed the action. As the man was being led away by the police, he became angry and started cursing at his mother. He thought she had turned him in to the police (and maybe she had). The cameras closed in on his mother's face, her expressions changing from sorrow to anguish as her disabled son was dragged away.

Then, she remembered his artificial leg. Knowing he would need it in jail, she quickly ran to the other room to get it for him. When she returned, her face was still filled with sorrow, but it also shone with a mother's love for her son as she stretched out her arm toward him, holding out his prosthetic leg.

I'll never forget his response, because his face turned even uglier and darkened with hate toward his mother. He refused to take the leg, and, as he was pushed into the backseat of the police car, he leaned out and spat at his mother. At that moment, her love was pure and sacrificial as she tried to help him at his lowest point.

He responded by rejecting her and her love with one of the worst insults he could possibly deliver.

What would you have done if you were that mother? How far would *you* go in order to love someone who didn't love you back? What do you do when you face rejection from the one you love? Let's see what God does when *He* is consumed by desire for those He loves, and follow Him through each stage as He handles the cycle of love given, rejected, and accepted with His people. Here's a hint—there was a time long ago when God's love relationship with His people involved a series of solemn vows and agreements called *covenants*.

## POINTS TO REMEMBER

- The love we feel for *things*, like a cell phone, a pair of designer shoes, or a fancy car, doesn't always last because material objects don't return our love.
- People were made to live in community and with connection, and we need to feel loved and connected every day.
- Relationships are the most important area of a person's life; they make us or break us.
- Every relationship you are part of influences you, lifts you up, or weighs you down.
- Three categories of relationships need to be in order for your best life: your relationships with others, with yourself, and with God.
- God offers His love to people. The cycle of His love often takes this form: love is given, love is rejected, love is accepted.

• God gives us His love because He *is* love. His feelings for people are like those of a passionate lover.

## QUESTIONS TO PONDER

1. People fall in love not just with people, but also with all sorts of things. What have you fallen in love with?

2. Amma is a spiritual figure who gives out hugs that make people feel loved. Do you recognize the need to feel loved in your own life? What sort of gesture makes you feel loved?

3. How are you doing in the three categories of relationships? Which category needs your attention right now: your relationships with others, with yourself, or with God?

4. Think about the cycle of love: love is given, love is rejected, love is accepted. Where are you in the cycle? Have you received or rejected God's love? How?

5. Have you experienced God's love in your life? Think of a time when you felt loved by Him.

# Who Is God Really?

*It ain't what you don't know that
gets you into trouble. It's what you
know for sure that just ain't so.*
—Mark Twain

Before you connect to Him, you first have to know who He *really* is. A fresh and true picture of God is available through understanding the covenants He made with humanity, including the "better covenant."

# CHAPTER 1

# Signed, Sealed, Delivered, I'm Yours

*Deep within every human being there still lives the anxiety*
*over the possibility of being alone in the world.*
—Søren Kierkegaard

As Søren's love for the lovely Regine grew ever deeper and stronger, he continued to write her beautiful letters. They were letters only a man in love could write.

"I am happy, indescribably happy, for I know what I possess. And when it storms and roars in the workshop of my thoughts, I listen for your voice," he wrote. "When I stand in a crowd amidst noise and uproar that do not concern me, then I see the open window, and . . . the distance between us vanishes and you are mine, united with me, though a whole continent were to separate us."[1] As with lovers since the dawn of time, Søren was inexorably drawn to Regine and wanted to spend more time with her.

Søren's heart belonged only to Regine, and he saw her face always. "Everywhere, in every girl's face, I see features of your beauty."[2] He also described her as his true north with his "I" magnetically pointing always to her, and said she "transfigured" him. His fantastical descriptions illustrated how he felt he'd found his heart's desire and soul mate.

Happily for Søren, Regine welcomed his attention and his visits, and, as lovers do, they began to exchange gifts. In one letter Søren said, "I am enclosing a scarf. I ask you to accept it and desire that you alone may know that you own this trifle."[3] Not only did he want to know that his gift was appreciated by her, but he asked her to keep it a secret between the two of them. The scarf was meant to serve as a visible and tangible proof of the growing bond between the lovers.

By paying attention to his conversation and his letters, it would have been easy for anyone to see Søren was madly in love with Regine. His words, whether spoken or written, clearly revealed his behavior and the passion of his heart. God's words are like that too. If you pay close attention, His passion for us is as obvious as Søren's for Regine.

The love, or lack of love, you have for someone is revealed by your actions toward him or her. The agreements God made with humanity flowed from His intense love for us. In the Old Testament, God's love was on display through the agreements, or covenants, He entered into with humanity. Part of the reason many people misunderstand God and His actions in times past is because they don't understand how God behaved in accordance with those covenantal agreements. The Bible is not just a story of religion or the history of God's chosen people; it is the story of God's love on display through His covenant journey with humanity. Throughout history God has been trying to lavish His love on His people, a love on display when He reached out to humanity and connected to them in a formalized way.

In the ancient world, when two parties made a covenant they would say it aloud, or write it and sign it, and the covenant would henceforward be legal and binding. There are three different types of these old-world covenantal agreements.

First is the grant covenant. A grant covenant is when a greater person and a lesser person enter into an agreement, with the greater one taking on all the obligations. The lesser one only needs to receive the covenant.

Grant covenants are also referred to as covenants of promise or unconditional covenants. God made grant covenants with Noah, Abraham, and David because He loved them and their families so much that He wanted a formal agreement to seal and signify their bond. In the biblical cycles of God's love given, rejected, and accepted, the grant covenants were God *giving* His love to His people and formalizing it with a binding agreement. God was doing all the work, and all the people had to do was accept the agreement and pledge themselves in a solemn bond to their Creator.

If you're a parent, you're familiar with this kind of relationship because you are in a grant-covenant relationship with each child. A newborn baby needs love, care, and attention to his or her needs twenty-four hours a day. As the parent, you plan and prepare for that baby, and when you finally bring that little one home, you spend most of your twenty-four hours a day thinking about what that baby needs and providing for those needs. For several years the work and the effort flow one direction. All the baby has to do is eat, sleep, grow, and develop. If everything goes the way it's supposed to, soon your little one is smiling and cooing at you as he or she learns how to return your love. That's about all you can expect for a while because a new baby needs to grow and develop before he or she can give back the love, affection, time, resources, and care you are pouring into the relationship. But as that baby grows into childhood, adolescence, and then adulthood, the relationship and the special bond between you grows too (especially if he or she learns how to be obedient, which seems to be harder for some children than others).

If you're not a parent, you can still see this kind of grant-covenant relationship in other ways. Perhaps you've been a caregiver, providing for someone close to you who has special needs due to illness, disability, or age. Many of us have cared for someone with different forms of dementia, including Alzheimer's, and as the dementia progresses the relationship becomes one-sided, much like a parent taking care of a young child. As a senior adult with dementia travels that long journey into the shadowy world of memory loss and confusion, he or she might forget not only names and dates but also how to get dressed or how to use a toothbrush or a knife and fork. As a caregiver, you step in and pour your love, affection, time, resources, and care into a relationship where you will not receive it all back.

If you've not yet been a parent or a caregiver, maybe you've been the proud owner of a pet. That, too, is a picture of a grant-covenant relationship. A new puppy or kitten requires a great deal of time and attention (not to mention money). As a pet owner, you're responsible for all your pet's needs. While it's fun to have a new pet in the house, it's also a tremendous amount of work, especially when it unintentionally destroys something or has an accident on the rug. Your puppy or kitten receives all your love and your care without even realizing the cost because you've taken on all the obligations.

In the grant-covenant relationship, God is the greater party and takes on all the responsibility. And here's the key—He doesn't mind, because He loves His people. From the beginning, He took the role of father and treated us as His children, making a grant covenant the best type of covenant. God wants to give His children everything He has.

The grant covenant between God and Noah came into existence after Noah and his family exited the ark after the flood. In Genesis 9, God starts with the command to "be fruitful and increase in number and fill the earth" (v. 1). Then He gives Noah a promise never again to destroy the earth by flood. He seals His promise with a rainbow, almost like Søren pledging his love to Regine with the scarf.

To understand the impact of this grant covenant between God and Noah, think about what Noah and his family had just experienced. Never before in the history of the earth had it rained, yet for forty days and nights it rained constantly. Every single person on earth, except for the four men and four women on the ark (Noah and his wife, and his three sons and their wives), perished in the epic flood caused by the deluge. Imagine the fear that must have poured into Noah's heart every time it began to rain after that.

While all their friends and extended family were dying, Noah's family was stuck on a boat with a massive number of animals, trying to feed and tend for them all. (That might make your own caregiving tasks seem not quite as bad, right?) The stress of this, added to the worry about what might happen next, must have been unimaginable.

But even so, Noah was faithful to the Lord. He obeyed and trusted God in a situation where he had no context—he'd never seen rain and knew nothing about boats or taking care of wild animals. But he believed God and was faithful to the Lord in a wicked world. It would have been much easier to follow along with the crowd of unbelievers and do what everyone else was doing. But Noah didn't. He believed God and so he stood out from the crowd, his belief saving him and his entire family. So God rewarded him with a grant covenant.

> God said, "This is the sign of the covenant I am making between me and you and every living creature with you, a covenant for all generations to come: I have set my rainbow in the clouds, and it will be the sign of the covenant between me and the earth. Whenever I bring clouds over the earth and the rainbow appears in the clouds, I will remember my covenant between me and you and all living creatures of every kind. Never again will the waters become a flood to destroy all life. Whenever the rainbow appears in the clouds, I will see it and remember the everlasting covenant between God and all living creatures of every kind on the earth."[4]

Even though Noah and his family had entered into a beautiful new covenant relationship with God, they still faced many challenges. When they did finally get off the ark and down onto dry land, the landscape of the earth had significantly changed. Everyone and everything they'd ever known was gone. It's difficult for us to imagine this sort of full-scale trauma.

Many of us are like Noah, having been through traumatic experiences that have led to fear and worry dominating our lives. But that's what makes the love of God so powerful through the grant covenant He makes with Noah. No matter what we have been through, or how challenging or devastating our circumstances, God promises to provide and take care of us. The covenant sign of the rainbow was a great comfort for Noah. Every time it threatened to storm or actually did pour down rain, he could remember the rainbow and know that God was still in control.

It's the same for us today. When a devastating hurricane like Katrina, Harvey, or Irma hits, or when a deadly tsunami wreaks havoc, God's love is still on display. We experience His love and care not only through rainbows, but through people taking care of one another.

In the same way that the people in Noah's time tried to live without God, one of Noah's sons named Ham, along with his descendants, attempted to do the same. God was simply not important to them. Ham and his descendants built the first high-rise the world had ever seen: a massive building known as the Tower of Babel. They wanted to build an empire and they wanted to do it on their own, using their newfound power for their own gain, so they rejected God's love and the grant covenant God had established with Noah.

Ultimately, the plans of Ham and his descendants were foiled. God confused the people by causing them to speak in different languages. They couldn't understand one another so they stopped building the tower, their superpower plans faded away, and as a result they scattered throughout the earth per God's original plan and direction.

God's disappointment in this group of people must have been

intense and painful. He had given them the earth to enjoy and repopulate, and instead they rose up and created plans of their own. They tossed aside the grant covenant God had put into place. Imagine if Regine had thrown the beautiful scarf Søren had given her in his face. Or as if your child, or your aging parent with dementia, who you've loved and cherished and sacrificed so much for as you've cared for all his or her needs, shouts hate for you. It's hard. It's painful. It's heartbreaking.

But all was not lost. Although there was an ungodly line of people who had disregarded the Noahic covenant, there was a godly line of people still on the earth. And one of those people was named Abram (also known as Abraham). He didn't know it, but he was about to join with God in another grant covenant.

This next grant covenant had even more incredible promises built into it—powerful and significant promises stretching all the way through the Old Testament and into the New. This grant covenant would change the fate of humanity with a completely new nation and a new religion.

## POINTS TO REMEMBER

- The love you have for someone is revealed by your actions toward him or her.
- The covenants God made with people, as recorded in the Old Testament, flowed from His intense love for us.
- In the ancient world, covenants were formal, legal, and binding agreements. There were three types of covenants.
- The first type of covenant was a grant covenant. In a grant covenant, God is the greater party and takes on all the responsibility, like a parent for a child.

- Perfection was not required from Noah; he only needed to trust God.
- God put the rainbow in the sky as a sign of His grant covenant with Noah and his descendants.

## QUESTIONS TO PONDER

1. Have you ever written or received love letters before? Did you keep them? Do you ever go back and reread them? How do they make you feel?

2. What kind of covenant agreements do we make today? Have you ever entered into a covenant with someone?

3. When God and Noah entered into a grant covenant, what happened with Noah's descendants that disappointed God? How do you think God felt when this happened? Did their behavior change the grant covenant?

4. Have you ever had someone reject a gift you've given? What emotions did it stir up inside of you?

# CHAPTER 2

# C'mon . . . Just Believe!

*We should not look back unless it is to derive*
*useful lessons from past errors.*
—GEORGE WASHINGTON

Young George Washington was known as a hard worker. George's father passed away when he was eleven years old, so young George knew he'd have to make his own way in the world. At the age of seventeen, he was already well on his way to success as a county surveyor in Virginia, and before long he saved enough money to buy some land of his own.

Years later after a distinguished military career, George married in his thirties and settled in for a happy period as a farmer. He became very successful, eventually increasing his land holdings at a place called Mount Vernon to more than eight thousand acres.

Then came the call to duty. Since he was successful, happy, and content, it wasn't something George was particularly looking for. Plus, he didn't really want to leave his beloved wife, Martha. But the colonies needed him in this important fight to birth a new country—the United States of America. For the love of this land, George answered the call.

In June of 1775, when George was forty years old, Congress commissioned him to take command of the army besieging the British in Boston. He thought he'd be back home in Mount Vernon by the fall, but he ended up serving, and serving well, for eight years. After this difficult task was done and he had resigned his commission, hoping to retire from the army for good, George was called on again to go to Philadelphia and head up the Constitutional Convention.

Yet again George tried to retire, but to no avail when he ended up unanimously elected president of the brand-new United States of America. His country needed him, and because he loved his country and he loved the people of his country, he answered the call by leaving Mount Vernon once again to serve as our first president.

Fortunately for America, he put aside his own interests to establish our nation when he would have rather been at home working on and expanding his farm. Because of his sacrificial service, his name has become synonymous with love of country, freedom, honor, and loyalty. George Washington sacrificed much for this fledgling country. He didn't have to do what he did; he acted out of honor, love, and a strong sense of calling.

The book of Genesis tells the story of a man much like George Washington. His name was Abraham (also known as Abram)[1] and he, too, had a successful farm. A few generations after the flood had destroyed the earth and construction on the Tower of Babel had been halted, Abraham was born in a land called Ur, located in modern-day Iraq. He married a woman named Sarai and eventually moved to Haran, in modern-day Turkey, where he became a wealthy landowner. He had great land holdings and vast herds of livestock, and he employed a large number of people. Running a large estate is like running a company, so essentially Abraham was an entrepreneur and the CEO of his own company.

Then, just like George Washington, Abraham got a call out of nowhere. The stakes were high, but it was a one-way agreement. God would be doing all the work.

> Go from your country, your people and your father's household to the land I will show you. I will make you into a great nation and I will bless you; I will make your name great, and you will be a blessing. I will bless those who bless you, and whoever curses you I will curse; and all peoples on earth will be blessed through you.[2]

Like George, Abraham was rooted and established, a man of the land. He led a community and poured years of his life, and all his passions, hopes, and dreams, into his business and his property. It was not at all easy to up and leave a place where things were going well to head out into the unknown.

How Abraham reacted to the call of God is surprising—no argument, no balking, and no excuses. The call came and Genesis tells us that "Abraham went, as the LORD had told him," taking his wife, his livestock, and all the people who worked for him and depended on him, and heading for the land of Canaan. The logistics of the move must have been overwhelming. There were no U-Haul trucks, no interstate highways, and no air-conditioned rest stops. This was a Herculean task requiring untold hours of logistical planning, hard physical labor, and unwavering commitment.

When Abraham and company finally arrived, they saw a beautiful new land, to be sure, but there was one little detail God had forgotten to tell Abraham. The land of Canaan was still full of its original inhabitants, a people called the Canaanites. If he didn't know it already, the difficult truth must have been hitting Abraham upside the head by now. Even though he was following divine orders, founding a new nation was going to be no easy task.

The promise God made to Abraham, and Abraham's response to God's call to move to a new land and start a new nation, constituted a grant covenant. Because God later changed Abraham's original name from Abram, or "exalted father," to Abraham, or "father of a multitude," this covenant is called the Abrahamic covenant.

The Abrahamic covenant is the second major biblical covenant and a significant milestone in the relationship between God and His people. When God called Abraham out and promised to make his name great, Abraham was busy doing his work, supporting his family, and building his business. He didn't ask to have a great name. The Lord just gave it to him. Abraham was the father of the faith because he started a new nation—one that would eventually become Israel.

As Abraham rebuilt his business and settled into his new community, he had many adventures, including a journey to Egypt to escape a great famine, various military battles, and a meeting with the mysterious king of Salem, called Melchizedek.

From time to time God spoke to Abraham and reminded him of the original promise. "Do not be afraid, [Abraham], for I will protect you, and your reward will be great," God told him in a vision. This time, though, Abraham answered God.

"O Sovereign LORD, what good are all your blessings when I don't even have a son?" . . .

"You will have a son of your own who will be your heir," the LORD said, taking him outside. "Look up into the sky and count the stars if you can. That's how many descendants you will have!"

Abraham believed the LORD, and the LORD counted him as righteous because of his faith.[3]

While Abraham was a hard worker and a good businessman, he didn't have the power and resources, or the blind ambition and ruthlessness needed to found his own nation. He simply was not equipped. Instead, the fulfillment of this second grant covenant was going to be God's doing and His doing alone.

It's like when parents make the decision to adopt a child—it's all on them. From the initial research and decision making, to the education, financial investment, endless preparations, the waiting and the wondering, and finally to the call and the beginning of the adoption process, the whole event is one-sided. The parents take on the work and responsibility, and the child is the beneficiary. If an international adoption is being pursued, the cost of time and resources is even more intense. But never does anyone expect a child being adopted to do an equal amount of work or invest the same time and money into the process as the adoptive parents. It's a top-down relationship.

Similarly, with Abraham God was taking on all the obligations, and Abraham only needed to believe God and receive the covenant. It was a solemn promise. "Because God wanted to make the unchanging nature of his purpose very clear to the heirs of what was promised, he confirmed it with an oath."[4]

While the covenantal agreement was clear to Abraham, the timing didn't seem to be. There was going to be waiting, lots of waiting, involved. Finally, because the fulfillment of the covenant seemed to be taking so long, and because Abraham was a man of action, he and his wife, Sarai, decided to take God's promise into their own hands and attempt to fulfill it on their own.

Abraham was a man of great faith, but faith doesn't mean perfection. It's hard to wait on God, and it seems woven into human nature to want to *do* something. So because Sarai was too old to have children, Abraham turned to fulfill the promise his own way, with a servant girl. He was impatient, and in a moment of weakness he abandoned God's plan and created one of his own. He must've thought he could speed up God's process with a little human help.

Sarai gave an Egyptian servant girl named Hagar to Abraham as a wife. The plan was for Abraham to sleep with Hagar and have children, and this part of the plan seemed to work. Hagar got pregnant, but the pregnancy generated extreme tension between Hagar and Sarai, resulting in Hagar's leaving and running away into the wilderness. Abraham's plan didn't seem to be working after all.

Then, miracle of all miracles, Abraham and Sarai had their own son, Isaac. God included Sarai in the covenant language: "God said to Abraham, 'Regarding Sarai, your wife—her name will no longer be Sarai. From now on her name will be Sarah. And I will bless her and give you a son from her! Yes, I will bless her richly, and she will become the mother of many nations. Kings of nations will be among her descendants."

Abraham was also renamed by God as part of the reaffirmation of the covenant. "I am changing your name. It will no longer be Abram. Instead, you will be called Abraham, for you will be the father of many nations. . . . I will confirm my covenant with you and your descendants after you, from generation to generation. This is the everlasting covenant: I will always be your God and the God of your descendants after you. And I will give the entire land of Canaan, where you now live as a foreigner, to you and your descendants. It will be their possession forever, and I will be their God."[5]

Doesn't that wording sound almost like a marriage agreement? You've probably heard it many times as it forms part of a marriage ceremony: "To have and to hold, from this day forward, for better, for worse, for richer, for poorer, in sickness and in health, until death do us part."

This agreement between Abraham, Sarah, and God was the formalization of the relationship between God and His people, whom He loved. And instead of a wedding ring, or a scarf like Søren gave Regine, God asked for a special physical sign of the covenant agreement—a medical procedure called circumcision.

> Every male among you shall be circumcised. You are to undergo circumcision, and it will be the sign of the covenant between me and you. For the generations to come every male among you who is eight days old must be circumcised. . . . My covenant in your flesh is to be an everlasting covenant. Any uncircumcised male, who has not been circumcised in the flesh, will be cut off from his people; he has broken my covenant.[6]

To be clear, the physical symbol of circumcision wasn't the qualification. The only qualification for righteousness listed thus far in Scripture was belief. Abraham believed the Lord and it was credited to him as righteousness. People who believed God were considered righteous, and the relationship was based on trust—the people trusted God to fulfill His promises to Abraham and to them.

Instead, the practice of circumcision was an outward sign or symbol of the covenantal trust relationship between God and His people, almost like a man having his wife's name, inside a heart, tattooed on his arm. Most people wouldn't see the tattoo, but it's precious to him, he knows it's there, and it's permanent. The tattoo is a pledge of his love for her. Likewise, the practice of circumcision was not the covenant or the relationship itself, but a sign and a symbol of that relationship and the faith in God that it represented.

At that point in the history of the relationship between God and His beloved people, the only standard of righteousness God required was belief in Him. For those early folks like Noah and Abraham and Sarah, their belief, faith, and trust in God were all they had. It was a true love relationship, with no set of laws needed at this point.

But this passionate love bond between God and His people and the closeness and intimate nature of that bond, as beautiful as it was, did not last. Humanity got in its own way and, tragically, love was not enough to see them through.

Love had been offered (by God to His people), and love had been accepted (by God's people), but that divine love was destined to be rejected. The grant covenants of Noah and Abraham were not going to be enough anymore. A new covenant was going to be needed, and it would be written in stone.

## POINTS TO REMEMBER

- God entered into a grant covenant with Abraham and his descendants.

- An outward sign or symbol of the grant covenant between God, Abraham, and his descendants was a medical procedure for baby boys called circumcision. The practice represented faith in God and His promise.
- The grant covenant was not based on Abraham's performance or perfection.
- The only standard of righteousness for Abraham was that he believed God.

QUESTIONS TO PONDER

1. How did Abraham react to the call of God? Do you think you would have reacted that way in a similar situation?
2. God wanted to formalize the relationship with His people, so He asked for a physical sign called circumcision. Today, some people get a tattoo or buy a ring or other expensive gift to show their love. What is an outward sign of love you have used to show someone how much you love him or her?
3. Have you ever loved someone so much that his or her behavior, and in particular that person's mistakes, didn't deter your love?

4. The only standard of righteousness during Abraham's time was belief. How does this fact change how you think God views you?

# CHAPTER 3

# Achy Breaky Heart

*Love is the eternal quest.*

—Jay McInerney

During the year of the engagement to his beloved, Søren stayed busy with his work. He got serious about his seminary studies, preached his first sermon, and wrote papers for his master's degree. But always, Regine was there stealing her way into his heart and mind. He wrote in his journal, "During that entire time, I let her existence entwine itself around mine."

Søren ended up writing thirty-one passionate and intense letters, and he gave Regine many gifts in addition to the scarf: flowers, lily-of-the-valley perfume, a music stand, a copy of the New Testament, a pair of candle stands, and a paint set. In his letters he called her "My Regine" and signed off, "Your S. K." He talked and acted as if he wanted to be with her for the rest of his life.

That is, until he didn't.

Unfortunately, after almost a year of engagement, along with passionate embraces, love letters, and wedding plans, Søren unexpectedly called off the engagement. Even though Søren had claimed to love her, in his journal he confessed that only one day after he'd proposed he had known it was a mistake.

It turned out that Søren was harboring major internal doubts about his suitability as a husband, and so he'd thrown himself into work as a way to avoid spending time with his so-called beloved. Less than a year after he had pledged his love and asked Regine for her hand in marriage, Søren broke off the doomed relationship and sent her a farewell letter, along with his engagement ring.

It was over. No more love letters. No more passionate expressions of his undying love. No more love story.

Regine was shocked and broken. There had been no warning. She'd believed with all her heart and soul the pen and ink declarations of Søren's undying love, and she had given him her heart. Only now Søren was giving it back, this time broken into jagged little pieces. After she read the letter she hurried to Søren's house to talk, but he was not there.

Love had been given, and love had been rejected.

*What happened to the passionate man who wrote those heart-wrenching letters?*

*Was it my fault?*

*Am I unlovable?*

*Have I done something to drive him away and destroy our love?*

*Is our relationship gone forever, or can it be resuscitated and rekindled?*

Still in love with her Søren, Regine left a note at his house pleading for him to reconsider.

The two did meet a few weeks later, and Søren confirmed his decision—he no longer wanted to marry Regine. Even though she was desperate and wanted him back, he made his feelings clear. The man who was once in love was now out of love.

You might know the feeling. If you've ever been dumped by someone you thought loved you to the moon and back, then you're able to imagine how Regine felt. The one who'd been pouring out his fiery love in letter after letter suddenly changed his mind, grew cold, and turned away. It's difficult to understand the whys behind an emotional shift like this, and this kind of complete and sudden rejection is a brutal blow to the one being rejected. "It will be the death of her," Regine's father said as his daughter grieved the end of the engagement.

The marriage was over before it had ever begun, and Regine's dreams of life with Søren were now nothing more than empty promises on crumpled sheets of paper. The bride never-to-be was forced to acknowledge the truth—the pledge was broken and she'd been completely and utterly rejected by her lover.

God knows that exact feeling all too well. After establishing His grant covenant with Abraham and blessing him immeasurably, several hundred years elapsed. Then, as a result of a famine, the Hebrew people of the Abrahamic covenant (and Abraham's descendants) began living in Egypt. They became known as "Israelites" after Abraham and Sarah's grandson, whose name was changed by God from Jacob to Israel. The people of Israel multiplied into great numbers, and millions of them were brutally enslaved by the Egyptians and began crying out to God for help.

At that time the Israelites' relationship with God was still based on simple faith and belief in God. No systems of law existed, and it would be 2,847 years before the law came into existence. The only standard of righteousness during this time was the same standard of righteousness Noah and Abraham were held to—a belief in God. All they had to do was believe in God, and He did the rest. The relationship was straightforward and simple—God loved His people and wanted them to love Him back. For a while they did and the people prospered.

By the time Moses rose as leader, there were upward of three million Israelites in the land of Egypt. The Egyptian king, Pharaoh, was worried about the vast number of people, so he tightened his power and kept them as a slave class with little mercy on their hardships. In response, with many miracles and demonstrations of His power and love, God raised a leader to bring the people out of Egypt and into the land He'd prepared for them. And so began the incredible wilderness journey of Moses and the people of Israel.

Yet even through this epic escape, and into the beginning of their journey through the desert, there was still no law. The people grumbled and disobeyed at times, but there was no written or formal set of laws, so there was no punishment for breaking laws. God's people still lived and operated under the original grant covenant between God and Abraham.

But all that was about to change. Exactly two months after the nation of Israel left Egypt under the leadership of Moses, they arrived in a wilderness at the base of Mount Sinai. Moses was summoned by God to climb up the mountain for a meeting. In this meeting God gave Moses the instructions on how the Israelites should prepare themselves to meet with Him. God yearned to be closer to all His people. God Himself spoke to Moses and said:

> Give these instructions to the family of Jacob; announce it
> to the descendants of Israel: "You have seen what I did to the

Egyptians. You know how I carried you on eagles' wings and brought you to myself. Now if you will obey me and keep my covenant, you will be my own special treasure from among all the peoples on earth; for all the earth belongs to me. And you will be my kingdom of priests, my holy nation."[1]

Once again and true to form, God was pledging His love to His entire special group of people. He had rescued the people of Israel from Egypt and brought them out as His chosen ones, His "own special treasure." He was in love with His people and yearned for them to love Him back. His desire for them was undiminished, although it has been hundreds of years since those first two covenantal agreements with Noah and Abraham.

After He met with Moses, God called on the people to come and stand at the foot of the mountain. It must have been an incredible sight with smoke billowing into the sky and the whole mountain trembling. But even through the lightning and thunder and clouds, God wanted His people to hear His voice for themselves. God loved His people desperately and desired a close relationship.

But there was a problem: the people were scared to death. "When the people heard the thunder and the loud blast of the ram's horn, and when they saw the flashes of lightning and the smoke billowing from the mountain, they stood at a distance, trembling with fear. And they said to Moses, 'You speak to us, and we will listen. But don't let God speak directly to us, or we will die!'"[2]

Fear was taking over and driving a wedge between God and His people. While God wanted the entire nation to have direct access—just as Adam and Eve had no barriers and no restrictions with God in the garden of Eden—it wasn't to be. The people were still slave minded and about to sacrifice real, authentic relationship for a set of rules carved in stone. Because they were too frightened to meet with God, they sent Moses to meet with Him instead. Their fear caused them to miss out on an incredible meeting with God.

The people's fear also drove them into dangerous relationships with other false gods. The people forgot their first love, or maybe had never known it, and before long many of them rejected God completely. They even went so far as to build a god in the shape of a calf and bow down to it. That shocking act of idolatry was utter rejection and sent a clear message to God.

*We don't love you. We don't want you.*

Can you even begin to imagine how God must have felt? He'd led His people out of Egypt, performing miracle after miracle and putting a brave leader named Moses over them as a guide, and still they turned away. They were bound by fear and couldn't clearly remember the God who really loved them with all His being. His heart must have been breaking just like Regine's. God, who had been loved wholeheartedly by Noah and by Abraham, was now being rejected.

In His wisdom, and out of a desire to stay in relationship with His people, God decided a new covenant was needed. A grant covenant was no longer enough to define the people's relationship with God. They needed something more detailed and with consequences attached. It was tragic, because God was offering relationship and the people asked for rules. It wasn't that God wanted a new covenant of rules and consequences. He wanted relationship, like in the old grant covenants where He took on all the responsibility. That was His heart. But it wasn't to be.

This next major covenant between God and His people would be a kinship covenant. A kinship covenant was different than a grant covenant, with each side taking on its own list of obligations. This type of covenant had a small set of obligations, and those obligations were evenly divided between the two parties.

A kinship covenant was also referred to as a "parity" covenant, meaning equal responsibilities. In keeping with what the Israelites requested, this kinship covenant was more about religion and rules since His people had repeatedly broken the grant covenants and worshipped other gods.

The kinship covenant was much more like a business contract. My wife and I have carried out some remodeling projects around the house, and with each project we sign a contract with the carpenter or craftsman. He agrees to do a certain amount of work to our specifications in a set amount of time for a set amount of money, and in return we agree to pay him for that work in a timely manner. Both sides have to agree and both sides have obligations to fulfill or else there are consequences. If the craftsman doesn't do the work well and on time, he doesn't get paid. If we don't pay him for his work, he can pull us into arbitration or take us to court. Both sides agree to abide by the rules.

God created the new kinship agreement because His people had rejected Him and His love and pursued relationships with other gods, through worship of and sacrifices to idols. If His people would accept the Ten Commandments given to Moses and agree to abide by those laws, then God would honor the new kinship covenant.

The kinship covenant forged with Moses, also called the Mosaic covenant, emphasized religion and rules more than love. It was more like a marriage of convenience than a passionate love relationship, and it required daily, ritualized sacrifices to atone for sin. To stay in relationship with His people, God became the partner and the punisher in the agreement. If the people broke the agreement there would be penalties. The people didn't understand that because of their slave-minded fear, they had sacrificed relationship and asked Moses to give them rules instead.

It was a huge shift and a tragic moment for Israel. God had offered a close, intimate relationship with His people and He was rejected. It was so terrible that in Deuteronomy 5:23–27, Moses retold the story forty years later to the children of those he led out of Egypt. The original agreement was broken and discarded, just like the engagement between Søren and Regine. Hearts were crushed and feelings bruised on all sides. A new relationship was needed, if there was going to be any relationship at all.

Strangely, after the dust settled with Søren and Regine's breakup, he asked to approach her to try to strike up some sort of friendship. The terms of their relationship had changed, but he wanted to stay connected somehow.

And so did God. Although His people had rejected that close relationship, He wanted to stay connected too. It wasn't the original plan, but it was still a connection. And it was now going to be the law.

The series of events surrounding the giving of the Ten Commandments on Mount Sinai marked a change. It is the first instance in the Bible depicting God's people so terrified of God that they ran away and refused to interact with Him at all. They stepped into the fear rather than stepping into the cloud where God could show them what He was really like. They rejected God's offer of a grant covenant in which every person could be a priest and they elected Moses as mediator. They chose rules over relationship.

The giving of the Ten Commandments was a kinship ceremony,

like a solemn set of marriage vows or a business contract. God really wanted a nation of priests who all had direct access to Him and represented Him to the rest of the world. He wanted a treasured possession and a holy nation. Instead the people asked Him for a kinship arrangement, like what they'd seen in Egypt. In reality, the grant covenant was too big of a blessing for this slave-minded people to comprehend or accept.

On that mountain, God famously wrote the Ten Commandments on two slabs of stone, front and back, creating a solemn contract. One slab of stone was God's copy of the contract, and the second slab was Israel's copy, in an old school way of creating a carbon copy.[3] Moses brought down the tablets and put both copies of the commandments in a ceremonial box called an ark, which became the ark of the covenant. The new kinship covenant was now in force and placed God in the position where He had to punish Israel whenever they violated the covenant. Unfortunately, this happened frequently.

The grant covenant God originally offered came from God's heart, while the kinship covenant of the law came from the people's hearts. That covenant did not fully represent Him or His heart toward humanity. It did not represent His interests or what He wanted to do on earth. Thus, the new kinship covenant and the law dropped a veil over God, disguising the true desires of His heart.

As a result, for the next thirteen hundred years, people were confused about God and His intentions for humankind. Many still are, because they look back at the law and how it was carried out and it obscures what God is actually like. This misunderstanding is why so many of us have, or have had, a wrong idea of God.

Throughout the tumultuous history of the people of Israel, God remained steadfast in wanting a relationship. He was, and is, in passionate love with His people, as flawed and fickle as we can be. But when He was rejected, He was willing to change the terms of the covenant in order to maintain relationship, although it was not His original plan. He never gave up on us.

## POINTS TO REMEMBER

- Søren seemed passionately in love with Regine and then unexpectedly broke off their engagement. Love had been given and then rejected. Regine was shocked, not knowing what caused the breakup. God knows this same feeling. He loved His people, but by the time of Moses their affections often turned to other gods.
- After God met with Moses on Mount Sinai, He called for the people to come and stand at the foot of the mountain. But the people were frightened and refused. Their fear got in the way.
- The Israelite people chose to worship a statue of a calf instead of God, sending a clear message of rejection. This led to a new covenant, called a kinship covenant.
- A kinship covenant is the second type of ancient covenant agreement. A kinship covenant is more about rules than relationship, with a set of obligations divided between the two parties. It's more like a business contract.

- The kinship covenant would be bound by a set of rules called the Ten Commandments. The new rules were written by God on stone slabs, with two copies.
- God never wanted to relate to His people through a set of rules, and this has confused people over the years. This misunderstanding is why so many of us have, or have had, a wrong idea of God as an angry old man in the sky who is all about rules and punishment. God has always wanted relationship, not rules.

## QUESTIONS TO PONDER

1. Have you ever had someone break off a relationship unexpectedly? In the aftermath were you able to move on quickly, or did it take time to recover?
2. The deepening of a relationship, whether a love relationship, a friendship, or even a work partnership, can be a little scary. Do you jump into new relationships, or are you more cautious?
3. The Ten Commandments are considered a moral code that many people still work hard to live by. Can you live all of them perfectly? Have you lived all of them perfectly?
4. Have you ever been afraid of God and run away from Him like the Israelites?
5. God wants a love relationship with you, not a rules-based relationship. How does that make you feel about God?

## CHAPTER 4

# Ugh! More Rules. Really?!

*There is only one happiness in this life, to love and be loved.*
—George Sand

In the good old days, to fly on a commercial airplane all you had to do was buy your ticket, pack your bags, and show up at the airport in time for boarding the plane. There were no lengthy security checks, no barriers or rope lines, no embarrassing pat-downs, and no X-ray machines. Friends and family could walk you to the gate or meet you at arrival with a smile and a hug. Flying was simpler and faster, and the planes came with more legroom.

Sadly, the golden age of flying came to an end when the attacks on the World Trade Center in New York took place. Airport security had already started to tighten up, but after September 11, 2001, everything changed. The federal government created the Transportation Security Administration (TSA), and travelers were introduced to a strict set of safety measures. TSA employees were highly trained and took their jobs seriously. As a result, many new rules had to be learned and followed before anyone was allowed to fly. While it was sometimes frustrating, the new security rules made citizens feel safe. With the events of September 11 still fresh in the nation's collective memory, Americans knew the rules were for our own good.

Then something strange took place: a disheveled man named Richard Reid boarded a plane for Miami on December 22, 2001. Reid wore a pair of bulky hiking boots with hollowed-out heels. Inside the hollowed-out spaces were plastic explosives. Reid's plan was to blow up an airplane with his shoes.

Since it had been only a few short months since the deadly attacks in New York, Americans were still very much on edge and alert to anything that seemed out of the ordinary. Consequently, when Reid pulled out a match during the flight and tried to ignite his boots, an alert flight attendant noticed and immediately called for help. The situation quickly turned into a brief but intense physical struggle, with other passengers helping to subdue Reid.

Ultimately Reid's terrible plan was thwarted, with the plane diverted to land safely in Boston. Reid was arrested, convicted, and sent to prison for life. Anxious fliers heaved a sigh of relief. Comedians made fun of him and dubbed him the Shoe Bomber.

But as a result of Reid's attempt to bring down a plane, yet another rule was added to the long list of security procedures. From that point on, all air-travel passengers were required to remove their shoes and walk through the screening process in socks or bare feet while their shoes were scanned for explosives. It was not an easy adjustment. It felt strange to take off your shoes in an airport, and the process slowed everything down as people struggled to untie, unzip, or unbuckle their shoes and pull them off while standing in line. Later, the rule was modified so some children, older folks, and prescreened travelers could keep their shoes on. But the point is, because of one person's attempted criminal act, another new rule was put into place for us to learn, remember, and comply with whether we agreed with it or not. Or whether we personally were guilty or not.

To this day the security rules continue to change, and every trip to the airport could mean another new screening method or a new item no longer allowed. Recently, there's been a rumor that travelers will have to remove all books from their carry-ons. We know the rules are there to keep us safe, but it's not easy to stay up on the details and remember every last little regulation—thus the water bottles, cosmetic containers, and pocketknives that end up being discarded at the last minute in the large garbage cans near the TSA lines. But as travelers we put up with the aggravation because we know it's for the best.

Our somewhat uneasy cooperation with TSA could be compared to the agreements God had with His people in the Old Testament. In the early years of flying, there was an unspoken agreement whereby travelers knew not to bring anything unsafe onboard an airplane, so the security rules were minimal. Travelers and the airlines had something like the grant covenants God had with Noah and Abraham. The airlines worked to keep everyone safe and the passengers didn't have to do much but show up.

But after September 11, the rules and procedures became much stricter. This new relationship between the TSA and travelers became much more like the kinship covenant God had with His people during the time of Moses, when God created a set of rules written in stone, plus consequences for breaking those rules.

God's original plan and preference for a relationship with

His people was not for rules and regulations but because of the people's rejection, and because of their unsafe and dangerous behavior, the rules were needed. Likewise, the airlines were also forced to create and enact a new system of rules through TSA because of safety issues; the government spends a great deal of money, time, and other resources to enact these rules and procedures and punish people who violate them, all in the name of safety. People who travel know that they must follow the rules or face punishment. It's a much more restrictive system, but for the most part it works.

But the kinship covenant God had with Moses only went so far. As Moses got older, he needed to pass the leadership of the nation over to a successor. Moses and God were kinship partners, and now that Moses was about to die, God was going to lose His covenant partner. So Israel supplied a new covenant partner—a man named Joshua.

Enter the vassal covenant. In the book of Deuteronomy, God instituted a new covenant with Joshua, and the new agreement was downgraded to an agreement called a vassal covenant. A *vassal* is a person who receives protection and land from a lord in return for loyalty and service. While a kinship covenant is between two equal partners, a vassal covenant is between a greater king and a lesser king. In other words, God and the new leader, Joshua, were no longer meeting on equal ground. The sad truth is, for forty years the people of Israel had done a terrible job of following the kinship covenant with God through Moses.

As a result, a whole new set of obligations were added, changing the covenant to a vassal arrangement. It's like the new TSA rule on taking off your shoes. Because of Richard Reid's dangerous behavior on that plane to Miami, the rules got heavier and more complicated. God's new vassal covenant with His people through His new leader, Joshua, meant extra weight brought upon Israel through the book of the law. God had always wanted a close, intimate love relationship with His people, but the people rejected Him and opted for rules instead.

The books of the law, Leviticus and Deuteronomy, have probably caused more people to reject God and descend into atheism than any other books in the Bible. Many people read the detailed, restrictive laws and think those laws show us what God is like. For example, someone might argue that God must be okay with slavery, mistreatment of women, and all sorts of other things that sound awful. Because of this misunderstanding and this false image of God tied to the vassal covenant between God and Israel in Deuteronomy chapters 5–26, people can develop a wrong perception of God and misread His loving ways. "Your God is a crazy person," they might say. "Look at these ridiculous laws."

But this is a mental disconnect because these laws don't represent God's heart or the original ideal. Some people say we need to instill the Mosaic laws into our government so we can apply God's ideals to our nation. But the Mosaic law is not God's ideal. His ideal is the way things were in the garden of Eden, and the relationships God had with Noah and with Abraham.

Yet during the kingly reign of a remarkable man named David, in the middle of the vassal-covenant era, humanity got a short taste of a different way of living and relating to God through a special grant covenant. David has been called a man after God's own heart and there's a good reason why. Besides being Israel's greatest king, David loved God with all his heart, mind, and soul. He wrote love songs to God that we still sing today. Those songs, the Psalms, are full of love and longing: "As the deer pants for streams of water, so my soul pants for you, my God. My soul thirsts for God, for the living God. When can I go and meet with God?"[1]

Here's a psalm where David pledges his love for God in powerful and emotional language, echoing the desires of God's heart:

> You, God, are my God,
>> earnestly I seek you;
> I thirst for you,
>> my whole being longs for you,
> in a dry and parched land
>> where there is no water.
> I have seen you in the sanctuary
>> and beheld your power and your glory.
> Because your love is better than life,
>> my lips will glorify you.
> I will praise you as long as I live,
>> and in your name I will lift up my hands.
> I will be fully satisfied as with the richest of foods;
>> with singing lips my mouth will praise you.
> On my bed I remember you;
>> I think of you through the watches of the night.
> Because you are my help,
>> I sing in the shadow of your wings.
> I cling to you;
>> your right hand upholds me.[2]

Don't these words sound almost like a love letter Søren would have written to Regine? Clearly, David longed for God, and he sounds like the ardent suitor in these verses; that's because his heart mirrored the heart of God for His people.

Because David loved his God way beyond a relationship based on rules and laws, God dialed back the vassal covenant just for him and created a grant covenant instead. The covenant between them wasn't based on David's perfect behavior, because he was far from perfect. He had many moral failures. If sin could have disqualified David from a relationship with God, then adultery and murder would have done that. But there was no disqualification because David's mistakes did not destroy his relationship with God. And neither will *our* mistakes destroy our chance for a relationship with God.

Since God's covenant with David was a type of grant covenant, it holds many similarities to the original Abrahamic covenant. As typical of grant covenants, it did not contain an "unless you screw this up" clause; it was unconditional.

But even more important, the covenant with David, like the covenant with Abraham, came with a promise: to bless all nations through his seed, meaning through his descendants. Likewise, the seed Abraham was promised was not simply talking about his own son, Isaac, but also the birth of the Messiah, Jesus Christ. So when Abraham received a covenant that promised to bless all the nations of the earth, that meant the covenant would divinely spread out and bless every single person on the planet.

This same concept exists in 2 Samuel 7 in the grant covenant between God and David. Although God was talking here about David's son Solomon in the immediate context, He was also speaking in a larger context about His son Jesus, who was both God's Son and the descendant of David.

The Davidic covenant stands alone and is very different in nature from the prevailing Mosaic covenant of that day. In the midst of the era of Israel's vassal covenant, suddenly David received a grant covenant, and it seemed to take place simply because his heart was right. He loved God with all his being. David seemed to know and experience God in a different way, and that close, intimate relationship David yearned for with God is another powerful picture of the relationship God wants with each one of us.

But David's love for God didn't make David a perfect person, and this was not to be a performance-based relationship. Far from it. David wasn't the best father and had problems with his children. He lusted after a married woman, took her from her husband and slept with her, then murdered her husband. In addition, his daughter was raped by his son and he didn't intervene. David's life, while it encompassed great success, was also characterized by a strong pattern of failure. Yet he was an amazing man in God's eyes. Why?

It's simple; David trusted God. He was looked over and passed over by everybody, including his own father, but God had His eyes on David the whole time. God was in love with David because, with all his flaws, David loved and trusted God. He was passionately in love with God. His failings never disqualified him from a love relationship with his lovestruck God. Their relationship was not based on an unattainable level of perfection on David's part, because David was only human. Like us, he couldn't be perfect no matter how hard he tried.

Instead, David's relationship with God was a picture of a new and different way of relating to God. A new covenant was coming. A better covenant. And that covenant would be built on a new law—the law of love.

## POINTS TO REMEMBER

- The Israelites didn't do a good job adhering to the kinship-covenant agreement they asked for with God, so the covenant was downgraded. The new covenantal agreement with Joshua would be called a vassal covenant.

- A vassal covenant was the third type of ancient covenant agreement.
- A *vassal* is a person who receives protection and land from a lord in return for loyalty and service. A vassal covenant is between a greater party (God) and a lesser party (people).

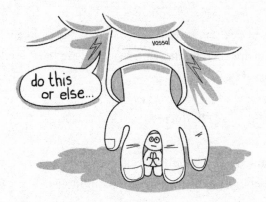

- The new, more restrictive covenant was needed because for forty years the people of Israel had done a terrible job of keeping to the kinship covenant with God.
- The new rules of the vassal covenant were detailed in the books of the law called Leviticus and Deuteronomy. Many people read these laws and think they show us what God is like, but these laws don't represent God's heart or His original intent.
- David was an exception. A man after God's own heart, David loved God with everything, so God dialed back the vassal covenant and gave David a special grant covenant, like He had with Noah and Abraham.

- David's relationship with God was based on love. David wasn't perfect, but he was passionately in love with God and trusted God.

## QUESTIONS TO PONDER

1. How do you feel about rules? Are you a person who likes rules and finds them to be helpful in your life? Or do you find rules restrictive and difficult to deal with?
2. Have you ever seen God as a rule giver? If so, did that make you feel closer to Him or farther from Him?
3. If you've ever read or studied Leviticus and Deuteronomy, you know some of the strange rules there. Can you imagine trying to live your life and keep all those rules perfectly? What kind of life would that be?
4. Why is David, a man who was chosen to rule Israel, and who wrote the book of Psalms, called "a man after God's own heart"?
5. What would it take for you to be called a man or woman "after God's own heart"?

# CHAPTER 5

# I Love You . . . This Much

*Never give up hope . . . love that has grown cold can kindle.*
—SØREN KIERKEGAARD

Once Søren and Regine's tragic engagement ended, Søren turned his passion toward someone new. But the object of his love was no longer a woman. The new object of his passion was God.

Søren had tasted the sweetness and beauty of romantic love with Regine, but he'd also felt like he could never be the man and the husband she deserved. As a result, he'd made the painful decision to break off the relationship and concentrate on his preparation to be a pastor and on his writing. While Regine went on to find happiness with someone else, Søren sought happiness with God.

Søren pursued his relationship with God with such intensity that much of his writing centered around the warm and personal love of God. Søren urged his readers to let go of empty religious practices to instead pursue a real, authentic, and tender relationship with a living, loving God.

In 1847, Søren wrote a book called *Works of Love.* "Deep within every man," he wrote, "there lies the dread of being alone in the world, forgotten by God, overlooked among the household of millions upon millions."[1] The answer to this problem of aloneness, according to Søren, was love. The most crucial part of life is *love* because love binds us to God and to each other and saves us from isolation. When we love God because He first loved us, then our lives will manifest this love and this kind of love will be eternal.

Søren's intense and lasting love affair with God reflected the same kind of relationship God had with Noah, Abraham, Moses, and David. Each believed in God, obeyed God, and loved God. They weren't perfect human beings by any standard, but each was passionate about his relationship with God.

However, the people of Israel were not always as faithful, falling into a repetitive cycle of love given (by God), rejected (by the people), and, finally, accepted (through a covenant relationship).

This cycle of love is on display in troubled relationships all around us, all the time. One person offers another person his friendship or love, but the other person isn't ready or willing to reciprocate with her love and the relationship falls apart. Sometimes, the one who rejected the initial gesture changes his mind and tries to revive the relationship, offering his love to try to resurrect the other's feelings. Sometimes it works, love is finally fully accepted, and the relationship grows into something beautiful and healthy. But sometimes it doesn't, and it turns into an unhealthy cycle of love offered and rejected on both sides, over and over, repeatedly hurting both parties.

Through these cycles with Israel, God maintained His love. He cared for His people, always desiring a close and affectionate relationship with them even when their hearts grew cold and their love for Him all but died out. God kept on loving His people. And, finally, after many, many cycles of love given-rejected-accepted, God sent to His people the ultimate display of His love and affection—His son, Jesus Christ.

Jesus' arrival on earth and what He accomplished here is the greatest demonstration of love the world has ever seen. Søren and Regine's passion pales in comparison. Jesus was and is the tangible expression of God's overwhelming, staggering, and outright crazy love for us. With Jesus everything changed, including the covenants. With Jesus there was a new covenant, a different kind of covenant. The writer of the book of Hebrews called it a *better* covenant than any that had come before.

With the arrival of Jesus, not only do we return to a grant-covenant relationship with God, where He does all the work, but the death and resurrection of Jesus is the greatest example of God's love the world has ever seen. No longer do people have to relate to God through a set of rules and laws.

The new era begins with the first verse of Matthew in the first book of the New Testament. "The book of the genealogy of Jesus Christ, the son of David, the son of Abraham," Matthew starts out.[2] Anyone with eyes to see can detect a close and specific connection between Jesus and the new covenant, and the covenants of Abraham and David. Jesus the Messiah was the son of Abraham and the son of David. In other words, Jesus was the living fulfillment of the promises made to Abraham and David.

When Jesus appeared on the scene, the people of Israel were still bound and living under the multitude of old, stifling laws and rules of the Mosaic covenant. The relationship with God must have felt like a whole lot of work, with failure to keep the laws inevitable. No human being alive could keep every single detailed law in the Old Testament Scriptures. Not only were the laws difficult to learn and to keep, but the religious leaders were constantly creating new rules, and new subsets of rules, for the people to obey. God's chosen people were relating to God in terms of obedience to an impossible-to-keep set of laws. Failure was guaranteed.

It can be the same today when certain churches or other religious organizations create sets of rules, and subsets of rules, for people to follow. Those who grow up in those kinds of restrictive religious systems sometimes picture God as an old cranky man in the sky making up rules and punishing people who don't follow those rules. Of course they do, if that's the only picture of God they are ever exposed to. But they're relating and responding to an old system. It's defunct. There's a game changer on the scene, and His name is Jesus.

When you try to live by the law, it never works. Here are the problems that I've seen crop up in a law-based relationship with God:

1. Performance based.
You feel like you have to perform, living up to the expectation of the law, or be punished. This creates a feeling that God will judge me, so I end up playing a role because my arm is being twisted to make me behave.

2. Fear of punishment,
If I don't perform properly, I'm afraid God will punish me and this fear makes me incredibly anxious.

3. Sense of inadequacy,
because I feel like I can go ahead and try, and try, and try again. But I will never be good enough to fulfill all of these laws to the letter.

4. Frustration,
because I'm forced to conclude I cannot comply. This leads me to want to give up, and results in a sure but steady drift away from God. I feel I can never be good enough.

With the new covenant centered around Jesus, we work from God's love; we don't have to work *for* it. Here's what happens in a love-based relationship with God:

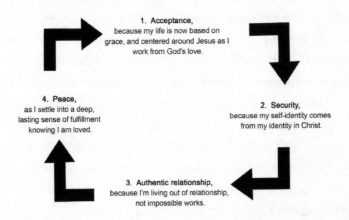

1. Acceptance, because my life is now based on grace, and centered around Jesus as I work from God's love.

2. Security, because my self-identity comes from my identity in Christ.

3. Authentic relationship, because I'm living out of relationship, not impossible works.

4. Peace, as I settle into a deep, lasting sense of fulfillment knowing I am loved.

Inspired by a diagram called "The Cycle of Grace" from James Lawrence's book *Growing Leaders* (The Bible Reading Fellowship, 2004)

The new covenant is based on God's love, a love that is powerful, passionate, unchanging, unending, and unconditional. The moment any person, religious leader, or system begins to put restrictions on God's love, he or she is heading down the wrong path, because there's a new path created by the life and work of Jesus.

There is a lot of power in how the genealogy of Jesus traces back to David and Abraham. He's the fulfillment of the promise made to Abraham and David—which is part of the reason why we have a grant-covenant relationship with God. The program changed with the arrival of Jesus, and the old ways of thinking about God and the system of laws would never be the same. Jesus' death on the cross and His resurrection removed the penalty and punishment of not living up to the law. When we're no longer living under the burden and conviction of the law, we can move on from the Mosaic covenant (the old covenant), and live and move and breathe in the new-covenant promise of a firsthand, personal relationship with God through Jesus Christ.

In this new covenant we're back to a grant relationship with God, where He does the work of forging a relationship with us because He wants our love. The new covenant under Jesus Christ is a whole new kind of law—the law of love. And that relationship is a face-to-face, intimate, soul-deep relationship. Jesus put on a human body with all its wrinkles and flaws and came down to live with His people in close community. What a contrast from God appearing in a cloud or fire, or staying up on a mountain and handing down laws.

Jesus' life changed the game once and for all as He lived and worked and socialized with His people. He loved His friends old and new and responded to everyone He met, rich or poor, slave or free, sinner or outcast, with the love of the Father. Jesus was God on display, living out the love of His father for all the world to see. Not everyone saw Him and accepted His love, but some did. Likewise, today not everyone sees Him and accepts His love either, but some do.

Although Søren gave up on his relationship with Regine, he never did give up on his relationship with God. Through his study and writing he came to a strong and abiding understanding of God's love and forgiveness. One of his most famous quotes is, "God turns sinners into saints." Kierkegaard knew well the cycle of love and rejection and in the end, God's love gave him hope where he once had none. "Never cease loving a person, and never give up hope," he wrote. "The bitterest enemy and also he who was your friend could again be your friend; love that has grown cold can kindle."[3]

Jesus is the ultimate demonstration of "never cease loving." He was and is the love of God given to us, and the love of God on display. God's love is for the entire world, and He gave His only Son for that world—the same world that had rejected Him.

God never stops loving us and never gives up hope that we will return His love. His love never grows cold. His love is always there, warm and waiting for an opportunity to rekindle the passion. Though we forget Him or push Him away, He is still lovestruck by us. And He always will be. We are desired by God.

## POINTS TO REMEMBER

- After the breakup Søren turned his attention to God. His intense love affair with God reflected the same kind of relationship God had with Noah, Abraham, Moses, and David. None of them were perfect human beings, but they were each passionate about their relationship with God.
- The people of Israel, however, fell into a repetitive cycle of love given (by God), rejected (by the people), and accepted (through the different covenant relationships).
- After many cycles of love, God sent Jesus Christ, His Son, and the ultimate display of His love and affection.
- What Jesus accomplished on earth is the greatest demonstration of love ever seen. With Jesus, everything changed, including the covenants.
- Because of the life, death, and resurrection of Jesus, we return to a grant-covenant relationship with God where He does all the work. We return to God's original intent.

- No longer do we have to relate to God through a set of rules and laws. Because of Jesus, we now relate to God through relationship. This relationship is not based on performance; as it was for Noah, Abraham, and David, it's based on faith and trust.

- Living a law-based relationship with God never works. Instead, with a new covenant centered around Jesus, we work *from* God's love; we don't have to work *for* it.

- Jesus is the fulfillment of the promises made to Abraham and David in the ancient but beautiful grant covenants. The new covenant under Jesus is based on a new kind of law—the law of love.

## QUESTIONS TO PONDER

1. If you've ever been rejected in a love relationship, how did you cope? Did you turn your love toward someone, or something, else?

2. Have you ever been in a cycle of love with God? Have you ever turned away from His love? What brought you back?

3. When you think about Jesus and His death and resurrection, do you see a picture of love in it?

4. Think about your relationship with God in the past. In your heart, mind, and spirit, did you operate more from rules and laws, or love?

5. Have you ever worked for God's love? What did you do to try to please Him? Do you think it worked?

# Love on Display

*Love is as love does.*
*Love is an act of the will—namely,*
*both an intention and an action.*
—M. SCOTT PECK

Throughout history, God has demonstrated His love for us through how He has revealed himself: His names and nature.

# CHAPTER 6

# Unconfined

*It always seems impossible until it's done.*
—Nelson Mandela

I want to tell you about two amazing people. Their names are Jim Abbott and Kris Carr. Once you get to know who they are and why they do what they do, you will never forget their names.

But first, I want to tell you about another name because it's the biggest, strangest, most complex, complete, unusual, unique, and unforgettable name you will ever hear. It's the name of God, the name that He called Himself 6,828 times in the Old Testament. God's personal name appeared for the first time in the book of Exodus, where God was having a personal conversation with Moses.

"If I come to the people of Israel," said Moses, "and say to them, 'The God of your fathers has sent me to you,' and they ask me, 'What is his name?' what shall I say to them?"

"I AM WHO I AM," said God.

*What?* Moses must have been thinking.

Remember, this was a direct conversation between the Creator of the universe and one single human being, Moses. He was afraid, insecure, and looking for confirmation and the right words to say what God has asked him to say. And God responded with, "My name is I Am."

*Huh? Say again?*

So God said it again. This time He explained a little more to the human shivering in fear in front of Him. "Say this to the people of Israel: 'I AM has sent me to you.'"

Moses must have been getting even more confused at this point. *What in the world does "I Am" mean?*

So God explained even further. "Say this to the people of Israel: 'The LORD, the God of your fathers, the God of Abraham, the God of Isaac, and the God of Jacob, has sent me to you.' This is my name forever, and thus I am to be remembered throughout all generations."[1]

It's hard to know if Moses really understood what God was saying, because it's not at all easy to grasp. But one thing is for sure: *I Am* is an unforgettable name.

Now, back to two other memorable names. You may have heard of Jim Abbott before. He was the first and only one-handed pitcher in Major League Baseball history. He was a first-round pick in the amateur draft and went straight to the California Angels without having to spend time in the minor leagues. And he could throw a baseball at ninety-four miles per hour.

Jim was born without a right hand, so when he was a child, doctors fitted him with a steel hook. At the age of five he took it off, tired of being called Captain Hook by the neighborhood kids.

His parents taught him how to tie his shoes with one hand (after they practiced it first), and then his dad showed him how to throw a baseball. Then he taught him how to switch the glove from his right wrist to his left hand fast as lightning to catch the ball, then switch it back again so he could return the throw.

His parents encouraged Jim to follow his dreams, then equipped him with the knowledge that he could make his dreams come true. And when he started pitching in the major leagues, it was a dream come true for fans as well. "He pitches his heart out every time," said Hall of Famer Rod Carew.[2]

Jim Abbott did not fit the stereotype of someone with a major disability. His talent, vision, and dreams could not be confined.

Neither could the life and dreams of Kris Carr, another unforgettable name. Kris was a young, fit, hardworking dancer, photographer, and actress in New York City. She worked on and off Broadway, plus did film, television, and commercials. She took good care of herself, including yoga workouts, but she got a call one day that changed her life. She was diagnosed with *epithelioid hemangioendothelioma*, a rare tumor attacking her lungs and liver. The cancer was stage four with no known treatment. It was incurable.

The doctors told Kris there were no valid treatment options, so doctors would be watching her closely for the rest of her life. "So you want me to *live* with this cancer all over my body?"[3] Kris asked. Her doctor said yes; even though her liver was covered in tumors, the hope was the cancer would be slow growing. Life had thrown her a challenging curveball. Kris knew what she would most likely eventually die of, but not when. So she made an important decision: she was going to live. Really *live*.

Fast-forward a dozen years and Kris is living her life with

energy, optimism, and a desire to help others. She's now a *New York Times* bestselling author, a motivational speaker, and a wellness activist for her own brand, *Crazy Sexy Wellness*. She wants to serve. "I have a mission to wake up, and to be happy and to take care of myself—and to teach other people to do that if they would like to."[4]

Kris's dreams and desire to serve come from her strong desire to live. Her cancer is not in remission; until there is a cure, she still lives with the cancer inside her body every day of her life. She carries it always with her. Kris's secrets are many: live healthy, be positive, cultivate joy and humor, don't be afraid to fail greatly, and the most important—"work from a place of love and compassion."[5] Like Jim Abbott, Kris Carr's dreams cannot be confined. She is the epitome of living life to the fullest.

Once you've heard their names and stories, or met Jim or Kris on a screen, in the pages of a book or article, or even in person, you will never forget them because they live unconfined, despite many significant challenges. Their incredible love for life is on display for all to see.

And, once you meet God, learn His name, and recognize His love unconfined and on display, you will never forget Him either. Learning God's name and understanding who He is will start you on a journey of getting to know Him in an intimate, unforgettable, and life-changing way. The names of God reveal everything about His nature, His being, His attributes, His power, and His glory. Knowing and understanding God's names will lead you into a deeper and stronger relationship with Him as you grow to know, understand, and love Him more.

"The name of the LORD is a fortified tower," says Proverbs 18:10. "The righteous run to it and are safe." The fortified tower is a beautiful idea and an enticing destination, but you can't run to it if you don't know more about it. You don't get to really know who God is until you know Him through His names.

One of the most unusual and hard-to-understand names of God is "I Am." God first revealed this name when He appeared to Moses inside of a burning bush. Moses had been living in obscurity, on the run for his life. Forty years earlier, he'd witnessed a fellow Israelite being abused by an Egyptian and tried to stop it, resulting in manslaughter. As a result, Moses had to flee Egypt, and he spent forty years in the backside of the desert. It was his first (and wouldn't be his last) wildnerness experience. He quickly found out how a harsh, dry, lonely desert can drain you of all self-sufficiency.

Perhaps you already fully understand how living in the desert can bring you to the end of yourself. Perhaps you've been in a desert in your own life, or you're in a desert right now. Take heart—Moses was there for a solid forty years before he met God in the burning bush. God is on His own timetable and sometimes He isn't in a hurry. Yet He wants to spend time alone with you, and that is worth waiting for.

This forty-year period for Moses turned out to be priceless. Those wildnerness periods are a critical and indispensable time for anyone who wants to be used by God. You need to know that God is all you need, but so many of us never get there until God is all we have. Being comfortable being alone with God is the prerequisite to being used by God.

After those forty years alone with God, Moses' antennae were up as he was listening for God, and he was sensitive enough to recognize God when He showed up. Moses was shepherding his sheep and noticed a bush on fire, but the bush was not consumed by the fire. Something strange was happening, and Moses stopped and turned aside to see it.

Had he not been sensitive to that "wait-a-minute" moment, he might have missed his moment with God. This is the problem with being so busy and consumed with life's dramas and details. When you let that current of busyness carry you along, it's so easy to dive into fix-it mode and miss a God moment.

And this was a God moment. Out of this profound experience, a one-on-one audience where God personally revealed His name to Moses, came an assignment straight from God. Sometimes we talk about a person having a sense of divine purpose, or feeling a calling. This moment between Moses and God was the definition of a calling, straight from the Lord.

But Moses felt like God was too big for him to understand, to explain, or to define to his people. He needed to get a handle on who God was in order to present Him and His will to the people, so he asked Him for His name. A generic sense of who God was—the God of Abraham, Isaac, and Jacob—was not enough for Moses. Because a name points to the nature, character, and essence of a person, Moses needed to know much more about who God was before he could do what God had asked him to do.

And the answer came when God said, "I Am." It was a declaration about who God is and what He means to each one of us.

God's name, I Am, points to the eternity of His being. In the beginning, and even before the beginning, God was there. He is without beginning and end. No created being can say this. Man has been created, but God is the Creator. When God says, *I Am*, He is saying, *I am in the past, I am in the present, and I am in the future.* God is timeless. There was never a time when God didn't exist, and there will never be a time when He doesn't exist.

*I Am* expresses God's existence in, of, and by Himself. We depend on Him, but He does not depend on us. God is the only independent Being in the universe. Everything alive depends on Him, but He depends on no one for life. He *is* life! He is unique among all beings in His omnipotence (all power), omnipresence (He is everywhere), and omniscience (all knowledge). These attributes make Him and Him alone the one true God.

*I Am* conveys the activity of God. The literal translation of *I Am* is *"I will be."* When it comes to His activity, He will be whatever you need Him to be in a particular moment. God cannot be confined to any particular role or way of acting or responding. He refuses to be labeled or pigeonholed. It's impossible to put God into a little box and to command Him what to do or how to do it. There's a danger in trying to confine and define God. You can't, because He is the great I Am. He will be all that is needed when the occasion arises.

*I Am* puts a declaration onto your situation. After Moses' meeting with God at the burning bush on the mountain, God sent him into Egypt and told him "I Am" sent him. The situation for the Israelites under the cruel thumb of Pharaoh in Egypt was dire and near hopeless. For four hundred years they'd been suffeirng and crying out to God. In response, God not only declared to Moses who He was, but He sent Moses back down into Egypt to declare His name and His identity to the situation. Moses was bringing the name of God, which is really a declaration of destiny based on God's promises.

The name of God is powerful and limitless, and when you bring His name into your current situation, you're making declarations that fly in the face of your present circumstances. When things look dire, the name of God makes a difference.

God will be what you need Him to be. When you're facing a desert situation or a situation of oppression, or when you're facing joblessness, homelessness, or friendlessness, or even if you're missing a hand or living a life with incurable cancer in your body, you can use God's name to make a change. "Let the weak say 'I am strong,'" wrote the prophet Joel.[6] The way you use His name brings consesquences. It doesn't matter how long you've been in that situation; what matters is what you say. So be sure to bring God's name into each and every situation, because in His infinite love for you, He will remove the limits that are holding you down.

*I Am* is a declaration about your own identity. When God first said "I Am," it sounded mysterious. But look at what God was doing; He was sharing His name with Moses so that Moses could then identify with, and be protected and nurtured within, that name. When Moses confronted the mighty and powerful Pharoah using God's name, I Am, he was protected and defined by God's name. This was new for Moses, as his previous identities involved being a part of Egyptian royalty and then branded as a criminal.

The truth is identity can be fluid, based on the information you have at any given time. In recent years, home DNA testing can sometimes provide surprising results, changing your ideas about your own identity. Now, for an affordable cost, you can purchase a home DNA kit and do a simple test to find out more about your ancestry.

This happened to a woman named Alice Plebuch, who took the test and received surprising results.[7] Alice had been raised by Irish Catholic parents, her father identifying strongly with his immigrant Irish background, but the DNA results showed her father came from a European Jewish bloodline. She was confused because she thought she already knew her roots. In addition, her parents had passed away and wouldn't be able to help her solve the mystery. She wrote the DNA testing company a letter complaining of a mistake.

But when a second test confirmed the results, Alice's curiosity sent her on a long journey of discovery because she felt like she no longer knew who she really was. Finally, after much research and effort, she found out her father had been accidentally switched at birth with another baby at a hospital in the Bronx. Everything she thought she knew about her father's genealogy was wrong. Reeling with shock, Alice realized she had a whole family she'd never met and knew nothing about. Her identity had changed.

Moses must have felt a similar sense of dislocation. His early life had been defined by his upbringing as an Egyptian prince, but God stripped him of that. He was no longer a grandson of Pharaoh. Then he'd identified with the Hebrew slaves and, in solidarity, committed a crime. But after his encounter with God, being a criminal would no longer be part of his identity either. His identity had been redefined as who he was in God. But Moses had to know God before he knew who he was.

Plugging into and drawing on God's power means we first have to know who He is. Power flows from His identity as I Am and then from our identity in Him. When we know who God is, we know who we are. We don't need to take a DNA test because our identity is solidly wrapped up in the great I Am and all limits are off. The apostle John put it like this: "You, dear children, are from God and have overcome them, because the one who is in you is greater than the one who is in the world."[8]

Here's the beautiful thing. Once you know who you are, you

also know who you are not. Because in and through God's power, you are *not*:

- worthless
- useless
- a has-been
- alone
- defeated
- trapped
- in despair
- without purpose
- without a future
- unloved
- uncared for
- unimportant

When you know God's name, you know who He is and you know who you are. When God sent Moses to free his people, Moses went to Egypt with a simple message: I Am. Whatever situation you find yourself in today, the message is the same. God is going to get you out of this mess, because of His name: I Am.

His name is the same in the New Testament, on display when Jesus' good friend Lazarus died an untimely death. When Jesus arrived on the scene, he was confronted by Martha, the grieving sister.

"If you had been here, my brother would not have died," she said. "But I know that even now God will give you whatever you ask." She knew who Jesus was, and she was asking for a miracle.

"Your brother will rise again," Jesus said.

"I know he will rise again in the resurrection at the last day," Martha responded.

"I am the resurrection and the life," said Jesus. "The one who believes in me will live, even though they die; and whoever lives by believing in me will never die. Do you believe this?"

"Yes, Lord," she replied, "I believe that you are the Messiah, the Son of God, who is to come into the world."[9]

*I Am*, said Jesus. Meaning, I Am here, I Am God, and I Am the One you loves you, who cares about you, and who came here to save you and your brother today and for eternity. *I Am the resurrection and the life.* And to show her, and the others who were watching, what He meant, Jesus went ahead and called Lazarus from the tomb, bringing him back to life, back into a sweet, beautiful, unconfined, and uncanny life.

When you know this I Am, when you really know and love God, His names, and His identity, you know your own identity and you are then empowered and set loose. Your identity has changed. Whatever situation you face, with your new identity you can walk out of the desert, stand up to Pharaoh, watch the captives set free, and enter the promised land.

Like Moses, Jim, and Kris, you can live unconfined. You can come up against obstacles and know there's a way. You can believe in yourself and do all things through Christ who gives you strength. All because you know God is the great, unconfined I Am.

## POINTS TO REMEMBER

- The names of God reveal everything about His nature, being, and attributes.
- Meeting God and learning His names will help you get to know how amazing He is and how much He loves you.

- God reveals His name to Moses as "I Am," and He said this is His name forever—how He wants everyone to remember Him.
- Moses spent forty years in the wilderness alone with God, and as a result he was prepared to listen to God and be used by Him. This intimate knowledge of God readied Moses to go to Egypt and face down Pharaoh for the freedom of the people of Israel.
- When you bring the name of God into your current situation, it makes a difference because the name of God is powerful and limitless.
- Moses' identity had changed from an Egyptian prince to part of the tribe of Hebrews enslaved by the Egyptians. His identity was then further refined when he learned who he was in God.
- When you know God and His names, your own identity is changed. You are empowered and set loose to live unconfined.

## QUESTIONS TO PONDER

1. Have you ever imagined what it would be like to come face-to-face with God, like Moses did? And to have a conversation with Him like that? What would you be thinking and feeling?
2. Have you ever thought about God choosing His own name? Does His choice of the name "I Am" surprise you? You have to admit, it's an unusual name!
3. If you could choose your own name, what would it be? Why would you pick that name?

4. Have you ever found out anything surprising about your own background? Did it change your sense of your own identity?
5. What is the point of learning more about God and His names?
6. What does learning that one of God's names speaks to living unconfined mean for you and your life?

# CHAPTER 7

# The Good Shepherd

*How gently did He gather me to Himself . . .*
—CHARLES SPURGEON

Names are important, not only to give you a way to remember and connect with someone, but you can often tell something about someone by his or her first, middle, or last name, or sometimes by a nickname. *Grumpy* might be someone to avoid in the mornings. *Princess* might require a good deal of attention. You most definitely want *Lucky* with you when scratching a lottery ticket. And *Sparky* might be the life of the party. A name often gives a clue to someone's nature.

My daughter's name is significant and important to who she is. Her name is Eden, which means complete, or perfection. But Eden was born severely premature. My wife had a condition called pre-eclampsia, a serious pregnancy complication that can threaten the life of the unborn child. We prayed for the birth of a healthy daughter, but Eden was born early and spent more than two months in the neonatal critical care unit fighting for her life.

Before I was allowed to hold her, I remember standing and looking down on her with all the love in my heart. Eden's tiny body was filled with tubes, she couldn't breathe on her own without oxygen, and my wedding ring could fit around her wrist. But to us, our daughter was perfect. We named her Eden, regardless of the outward circumstances. Her name was based on her nature. Despite her size or her health, to us she was perfection, like the garden of Eden God had created for His beloved people. We loved Eden without regard to the challenges or obstacles she faced. Her name was who she was, and Eden was our love on display.

But the story was a little different for another married couple I read about. When this couple found out they were pregnant, they decided to pick an exotic name for their unborn baby, so they chose the name *Ottilie*.[1] The unusual name, of German origin, was pronounced "OTT-eh-lee."

But once Ottilie made her debut and the parents began to introduce their precious little daughter to friends and family, the problems started. Somehow, when people tried to pronounce the unfamiliar name, the double T's sounded more like D's, and her name would come out sounding like *Oddly*. Needless to say, her parents quickly changed her name to Margot, a name much more familiar to everyone.

In biblical times, names were often profound, pointed descriptions of someone's character, sometimes handed down by God Himself. Noah's name meant "rest" or "comfort" in the Hebrew language, a hint of the safe place God would provide for him and his family inside the ark. Abraham's name meant "father of many," which tied into the promises God gave him. The name David meant "Beloved," a fitting description of a lowly shepherd boy who would grow up to be a king and a man after God's own heart.

One of God's names that reveals so much about who He is and how He feels about us comes from Psalm 23, a song written by David that portrays God as the Good Shepherd. As you know if you've ever seen one, a shepherd tenderly and tirelessly cares for his sheep as carefully as if they were his own children. At his core, a shepherd loves his sheep.

During a recent trip to Jerusalem, I saw a flock of goats on the side of a hill. The goats were scattered about doing what goats do—eating anything and everything within reach. I'm assuming the property owner had hired the goatherd and his flock of goats to mow down the greenery on the hillside to keep the vegetation under control. As I passed by, I caught a quick glimpse of a man standing in the center of the flock. The goatherd was an older man with a white beard, and he stood quietly, his eyes scanning the flock with a look of intense concentration. The flock was his, and they grazed peacefully while he watched over them. It was a scene of perfect harmony.

David had firsthand experience and knew exactly what he was talking about when he wrote this psalm, because he grew up a shepherd, tending to his father's sheep:

> The LORD is my shepherd; I shall not want.
> He makes me to lie down in green pastures;
> He leads me beside the still waters.
> He restores my soul;
> He leads me in the paths of righteousness
> For His name's sake.

Yea, though I walk through the valley of the shadow
of death,
I will fear no evil;
For You are with me;
Your rod and Your staff, they comfort me.
You prepare a table before me in the presence of
my enemies;
You anoint my head with oil;
My cup runs over.
Surely goodness and mercy shall follow me
All the days of my life;
And I will dwell in the house of the LORD
Forever.[2]

While David had been a shepherd as a young boy, he penned this psalm later in his life as a reflection of who God was, based on walking and working with God for much of his life. He knew beyond a shadow of a doubt that the Lord was like a shepherd. The Lord was *his* shepherd.

A comparison of God to a shepherd had been used before. When Jacob, one of the patriarchs of the Bible, was getting ready to die, he blessed his son Joseph and said, "May the God before whom my fathers Abraham and Isaac walked faithfully, the God who has been my shepherd all my life to this day . . ."[3]

In the New Testament, Jesus used this same description for Himself. "I am the good shepherd," He said. "The good shepherd lays down his life for the sheep."[4]

Throughout the Old Testament, God revealed Himself as a shepherd, and in the New Testament, Jesus revealed Himself as the Good Shepherd. This is what God showed us and it's who He is.

But it's also who we need to allow Him to be, because a shepherd leads and his sheep follow. We as sheep are supposed to follow our Shepherd, but that's not always what happens. Sometimes we have a tendency to want to get ahead of our Shepherd and that can be a dangerous place to be.

A friend told me a story about a man who purchased a new Labrador Retriever puppy. The man loved to hike in the mountains, and as soon as the puppy was old enough, he started taking it with him on the steep and winding trails. Some of the hikes involved switchbacks, with the trail undulating back and forth in an S pattern. The puppy sometimes got excited and charged ahead, and the man soon noticed if the trail curved, the puppy would go straight, completely missing the turn and heading off into the brush.

The puppy was too young and inexperienced to understand how to stay on the trail and follow the twists and turns on its own. As long as the puppy followed the man, it was safe. But when it got ahead of the man, it ended up straying off the trail and heading into danger. Out in the wilderness, the puppy could get lost and be vulnerable to predators. It was crucial for the puppy to learn to follow the man, because he knew the right way to go and would keep them both safe on the trail.

We can be like that headstrong puppy, getting ahead of our shepherd and heading into danger by getting off the trail. God is our Good Shepherd and wants us to get to know Him and allow Him to lead us as Shepherd.

The shepherd is gentle. He doesn't drive the sheep, but he leads them. God loves us too much to push us and force us. He doesn't coerce us, He leads us. I still remember singing in the children's choir at my childhood church in Atlanta and singing that sweet old hymn, "Lead Me, Guide Me." He is leading, and it's up to us to follow. He is the Shepherd, and whether you acknowledge Him as Shepherd or allow Him to be Shepherd, it doesn't change the fact that He *is* the Shepherd. Nothing you believe or don't believe changes this core facet of His identity.

If we follow the Shepherd and trust the Shepherd, He will meet our every need no matter the circumstances. In that first line, "the LORD is my shepherd," David used a particular Hebrew word for Lord: *Jehovah.* This name points to the covenant promises of God with Abraham in Genesis 15. David was talking about the covenant-making God who makes and keeps His promises. Jehovah is a God you can trust, and Jehovah is "my shepherd."

The role of a shepherd is to guard the sheep, lead the sheep, provide for the sheep, take care of the sheep, rescue the sheep, and love the sheep.

When the sheep need food, the shepherd provides it.
When the sheep need water, the shepherd finds it.
When the sheep need rest, the shepherd plans for it.
When the sheep need healing, the shepherd assists with it.
When the sheep need direction, the shepherd is ready for it.

Whatever the need, the shepherd provides. That's what David was saying—God is adequate for any and every need the sheep might have. That means when we trust and follow the Good Shepherd, we will have everything we need and we'll never lack the necessities of life. This is why David said, "I shall not want." We shall not be in need because the job of the shepherd is to provide for the sheep. The Lord has everything we need, but we have to let Him lead and we have to stay in the pasture.

When we stay in the pasture, there are some important and beautiful benefits. "He makes me to lie down in green pastures; He leads me beside the still waters." Sheep won't lie down and rest when they're hungry—they keep going, wandering and hungry and searching for their next meal, and sometimes not even realizing the green pasture is where they already are. The Good Shepherd leads us to the best pastures and makes us rest because we're already in the best place, but if we keep going, we're liable to walk right past it, looking for something we already have.

Sheep won't drink from fast-flowing streams because they're fearful of the sound and fury of quick-moving water. So when the shepherd knows the sheep are thirsty, he leads them to still waters by damming the waters upstream, slowing the water down and creating calm places where the sheep can drink. Could it be that's what God is doing in your life right now? He's upstream slowing down the flow of your life so you can rest and be restored? Sometimes we get in a big hurry and want everything to happen right now, right here, but that's not how your soul is restored. The Good Shepherd sometimes makes us rest and causes the stream to slow down, so that He can put us into a calm, peaceful, refreshing place to restore our souls.

When we're rested and ready to move to a new pasture, God leads us in the paths of righteousness. Those paths are well-worn paths. Whenever sheep start exploring their own paths and breaking trail without the shepherd's guidance, they get into trouble. Those new paths might include troubled places in marriage, family, finances, and relationships. So the Good Shepherd leads His flock along well-worn paths that the Shepherd has been down before, on well-worn paths like holiness, character, fidelity, faithfulness, family, truth, love, sacrifice, and honor. Those are the paths He wants us to walk on and stay on.

Not long ago, a well-known NBA player who played for the New Jersey Nets and the Milwaukee Bucks was sentenced to nine years in prison for defrauding other basketball players in a real estate scheme. Over a period of years, he'd been collecting money for real estate investments that never panned out, and finally the law caught up with him. He proclaimed his innocence, but the evidence told another story. At some point, even though he had a promising career in basketball, he missed the right turn and left the path he was on for a different path, one that led him into danger.

The Good Shepherd wants us to stay on those safe paths of righteousness "for his name's sake." As His sheep, we carry His name. As a father, I understand this because my kids carry my name. My name is on them. Before we ever go out in public, I share a few "encouraging words" with my kids about how I expect them to behave because I want to be as proud of them in public as I am at home. My kids reflect my name just as the sheep reflect the shepherd's name.

While the shepherd's role is crucial in leading the sheep to rest, to eat and drink, and to walk on the right path, it's even more important in difficult, frightening life situations. When the sheep walk through the valley of the shadow of death, the shepherd is there. Sheep aren't known for their sharp eyesight, and so they are easily spooked in new situations, especially when it's dark. What gives them peace and comfort is knowing the shepherd is there. In this psalm, David was telling God, "even though I've been through some really difficult stuff, I knew I was going to make it because I know You are with me!" When my wife and I had to walk through the valley of death with Eden's premature birth and the complications that she had to struggle through, we knew God was in the lead and He was walking us through. The Good Shepherd was in the valley with us, not watching from somewhere outside or in the distance.

It's like the difference between a firefighter and a fire inspector. The fire inspector checks out the building to make sure the exits are adequate and clearly marked, the building is up to code, and the fire sprinklers are working. But he leaves well before any fire ever starts. It's the firefighters who are there when the building catches on fire. God is like the firefighter who runs into the building to save and rescue when everyone else is running out. He gets in the fire with us when we need Him. That's what you do when you're crazy in love with someone—you get in the fire. You walk through the valley of the shadow of death with the one you desire. And the closer we get to the Good Shepherd, the safer we are and the more His peace will fill our hearts. We can handle the dark and the fire when we know He is there.

When David said, "You prepare a table before me in the presence of my enemies," he wasn't talking about a physical table. The city of Jerusalem is set on hills, and the flat places in the hilly terrain were called *tables.* At the end of the day, the shepherd would lead the sheep into the sheepfold on a flat surface called a table. The fold was surrounded by a stone wall and there was an opening. In that opening the shepherd would lie down and sleep, keeping the sheep from wandering out and any predators from stealing in. "I am the gate," said Jesus. "Whoever enters through me will be saved. They will come in and go out, and find pasture."[5]

During the night, thieves and dangerous animals like wolves or big cats could approach the sheepfold, but there was no way they could reach the sheep. They could pace outside the fold and watch the sheep rest safely inside, but they couldn't get past the shepherd at the door. God might not remove every danger or difficult issue from our lives, but we're safe inside the fold. No enemy can get to us because they can't get through the Good Shepherd.

As the sheep lie down to rest for the night, and as the shepherd attends to any wounds and injuries by anointing them with olive oil, the sheep might well reflect back over the course of the day. Perhaps they remember the fresh, tasty grass and the cool, clear water the shepherd had led them to, much as we might lie in bed and thank God for His protection and provision up and down the hills and valleys of life. As His sheep, we have been blessed by the Lord with goodness and mercy, and He desires every good thing for us.

For now and for always we have everything we need from the Good Shepherd, who loves us and wants us to be safe. As we learn His voice, follow His leading, and stay on the right path, we will be right in the middle of His care. We are His sheep, we carry His name, and He carries us in His heart.

## POINTS TO REMEMBER

- In biblical times, names were often profound, specific descriptions of someone's character.
- Another one of God's names is the Good Shepherd. A shepherd tenderly cares for his sheep as carefully as if they were his own children.
- Jesus called Himself the Good Shepherd, who lays down His life for the sheep.
- Since we are His sheep, we need to get to know Him and His voice, and allow Him to lead us. In doing that, He will meet our needs.
- The Shepherd wants us to stay on the safe paths of righteousness. This is so important in difficult, frightening life

situations. Likewise, during the night, the sheep are safe in the fold with the shepherd guarding the door so no enemy can get in.

- We have everything we need from the Good Shepherd, who loves us and wants us to be right in the center of His care.

## QUESTIONS TO PONDER

1. Have you ever been given a nickname? How did you feel about it? Do you think it fit you?
2. Isn't it comforting to know God loves us enough to lay down His life for us? Have you ever loved someone enough to put your life in danger to protect him or her?
3. Do you feel as if you are getting to know and recognize the voice of God in your life? What are some ways you can become more familiar with His voice?
4. Are you a person who tends to stay on the right path? Or are you more of an adventurous person, who likes to stray from the path and explore?
5. Do you feel safe when you sleep at night? Does it make you feel safer to know the Good Shepherd is watching over you at night when you sleep?
6. Does the description of God as Shepherd resonate with you? If so, how?

# CHAPTER 8

# The Fixer

*The wilderness is healing, a therapy for the soul.*
—Nicholas Kristof

It started out as a simple date—a hike in the Southern California sunlight. Brandon and Gina were both in their twenties when they met on a social media site and quickly hit it off. On their fifth date, they decided on an outdoor adventure just outside of Palm Springs, California—a scenic tram ride to the top of San Jacinto, Southern California's second highest peak at 10,804 feet.[1]

At first, everything went well as the couple hiked around the top of the mountain. But within a couple of hours, Brandon and Gina left the trail and headed down a canyon, hoping to see a waterfall they thought they heard in the distance. They never found the waterfall, but after a few hours they did discover they couldn't get back up the steep trail and realized they were going to have to spend the night outside. All they had with them was a camera, lip balm, a tiny tube of sunscreen, and two pieces of gum. They had no water, no food, and no extra clothing.

The temperature dropped to forty degrees that night, and they huddled together between some rocks, trying to stay warm. They didn't sleep much. The next day, they continued hiking down the mountain, hoping search parties would be out looking for them soon. But they saw no one, and they began to wonder if they were going to make it out alive.

Have you ever felt like Brandon and Gina? Wandering in the wilderness, not knowing which way to go, and hoping that somehow, someway, help is coming?

God's people felt like that after God brought them out of Egypt. They had been rescued from slavery, saved from Pharaoh and his army, and ushered through the Red Sea on dry ground with Moses as their leader. When they were finally safe and out of Egypt, the people knew God had intervened, and they erupted into a huge celebration of praise. With Moses and his brother Aaron and sister Miriam, the millions of newly free people of Israel sang songs, played their tambourines, and danced. It was a good old-fashioned praise party as they celebrated the God who had listened to their cries for help and who cared enough to intervene.

When the party was over, Moses led the people of Israel away from Egypt and the Red Sea and out into the desert. The mass of people walked for three days without finding water. Finally, they arrived at a place called Marah. There was plenty of water, but there was a problem because the water was too bitter to drink.

As the echoes of the praise party faded away into the dry desert air, the people began to complain about their three long days in the wilderness. It was hot and dusty and they were tired. And thirsty. They turned to Moses demanding, "What are we going to drink?"

Desperate, Moses cried out to the Lord, and the Lord showed him a tree. The tree was the solution. It had already been there, but Moses didn't notice it until God showed it to him. As instructed, Moses took a branch of the tree and threw it into the water, and a miracle occurred—the waters were made sweet and the people could drink. The oasis that had merely looked like a place of refreshment now became one, and the people had as much fresh, clear water as they could drink. They were saved.

But God needed His people to understand something. He wanted to reveal a crucial and important part of His nature, so "He made a statute and an ordinance for them, and there He tested them, and said, 'If you diligently heed the voice of the LORD your God and do what is right in His sight, give ear to His commandments and keep all His statutes, I will put none of the diseases on you which I have brought on the Egyptians. For I am the LORD who heals you.'"[2]

What does it mean to be a healer? To be a healer means to be a fixer. A healer is a person who can cure a disease or injury, or who mends or repairs something. And that describes just about all of us. Every single one of us is broken and in need of mending, if not physically, then emotionally, mentally, or spiritually. We are each of us, in our own way, diseased. The word *diseased* sounds terrible, doesn't it? When I hear the word *disease*, I can quickly conjure up awful images of damaged flesh or broken bones. But at its core, *disease* simply means *"dis-ease,"* or something that causes distress or anguish.

Dis-ease can be anything from physical illness to mental illness, grief at the loss of a loved one or disappointment in a failed relationship, difficulties at work or financial struggles, or any of a thousand other problems. Life can sometimes feel like a long string of unexpected challenges, and we're left in the wake, struggling to stay afloat. We need a life jacket and a helping hand to recover from these bumps and bruises that leave us feeling tender and sometimes feeling scarred. We've all been there. Michael Hyatt once said we're either in a crisis, just coming out of a crisis, or about to go into a crisis. Life doesn't happen without problems—it happens in the midst of those problems. And when we're walking with the Lord, those problems should drive us to our knees to ask Him for help. The truth is, to live out the abundant life God has promised, we need a fixer and a healer. God is the one who can rescue us, fix us at all levels, and heal us from our dis-ease. Anything else is a temporary Band-Aid.

With the story of Moses and the branch comes the first mention of healing in Scripture, and it's a clue to the identity and nature of God. He was revealing an important part of who He is—a God who loves His people and who is pledging to keep them from disease. God is the healer who can lead you through a bad situation and into a land flowing with milk and honey. God did it for the nation of Israel, and He does it in the life of anyone who commits to living for Him. The wilderness is school, a season when God is molding you, shaping you, and preparing you for what He is bringing you to. There is a purpose for the trek through the wilderness. You cannot step into the bountiful land He has prepared for you without having gone through the wilderness, because without the wilderness you won't be ready for the land.

This process takes time. We want God to turn our circumstances around quickly. We want God to take us from no place to the best place. When your wilderness experience hits, you might wonder if you're good enough, if you're headed in the right direction, and if you have the strength and resolve to endure. We want

God to make the situation perfect and easy overnight, but God doesn't work like that. Tests and trials in a wilderness season means God is shaping you and molding you for what lies ahead. Nothing is wrong—you're just going through your wilderness season.

This jaunt into the wilderness was not a mistake on God's part for the people of Israel. There was no miscalculation in the navigation system. God was deliberately leading them into the wilderness because He knew His beloved people needed challenging new experiences in order to grow and mature and really get to know Him.

Back on that rugged mountain in California, Brandon and Gina had to start working together even though they barely knew each other. They gathered rocks and made a big X on the ground, hoping searchers would see it. They created a mantra and kept repeating it together: "We are not dying on this mountain."

After a boulder almost crashed down on Brandon, they learned to stay close together to avoid causing rockslides that might injure each other. They encouraged each other, vowing to stay strong and get out of the wilderness. They were facing a huge test of their new relationship and learning much about each other and themselves. Trials have a way of revealing the contents of the human heart.

The people of Israel's reaction to their test at Marah clearly revealed the condition of their hearts. As soon as they ran into a problem, they began to complain instead of trust God. Instead of asking, "How is God going to do this?" the question was, "What are we going to drink?"

Because He cares, God allows us to come to places of testing to see if we will trust Him. Based on previous miracles, we should! The people of Israel had experienced incredible miracles of deliverance a few days prior, but somehow their trust in God had already faded. Yet they were traveling under the leadership of a God who loved them, who was watching over them and taking care of them, and who was their healer.

"Do not worry about your life, what you will eat or drink; or about your body, what you will wear," said Jesus. "Is not life more than food, and the body more than clothes? Look at the birds of the air; they do not sow or reap or store away in barns, and yet your heavenly Father feeds them. Are you not much more valuable than they? Can any one of you by worrying add a single hour to your life?"[3]

If God takes care of the birds and the flowers, caring for them by feeding them and healing them, He will certainly take care of His people. God allows us to come to places of testing to see if we will trust Him, but so often we don't. So the Lord tests us by sending us into the wilderness to encourage spiritual growth and to bring the best out of us.

The attitude we take toward the test and the challenges will determine what direction in life we go. What life does to us depends on what life finds in us. When these situations come, if we trust God, we will pass the test and grow. But if we mumble, grumble, and complain, we will fail the test and remain right there. Complaining never solves the problem. If all you do is complain and run away, you'll take the same bricks you carried with you out of Egypt into a new situation, and ultimately build for yourself the identical house you lived in as a slave in Egypt. Instead, those bitter situations of life, like the bitter waters of Marah, are designed to drive us to the Lord. He wants us to cry out for Him, not complain about Him.

On their fourth day in the wilderness, Brandon and Gina came upon an old, abandoned campsite. Among the weathered gear, they found a backpack with some maps, medicine, socks, and other supplies inside. They had no idea what happened to the camper or why he'd abandoned his camp, but they were grateful for the unexpected provisions.

As they went through the backpack a second time, they saw something they'd missed before—a package of fireproof matches. What if Brandon gathered some dry brush and logs and started a bonfire? The smoke might send a message to their potential rescuers. They still had no idea if anyone was looking for them, but they hoped a fire would draw someone's attention.

After four days of no food and little rest, the couple had little strength left, but somehow Brandon found the energy to gather enough wood to use the matches they'd found to start a fire. It quickly caught and even spread to some trees nearby, with thick black smoke billowing up into the air. Surely rescue would be coming soon, the desperate couple thought.

Finally, a rescue team spotted the smoke. Even though the fire had burned itself out within forty-five minutes, the smoke had been sighted and a helicopter was on the way. The unexpected matches in the backpack they'd found saved the lives of Brandon and Gina.

Not only does a period in the wilderness show us something about ourselves, but the experience gives us an opportunity to learn the abundance of God's provision. We never have the opportunity to experience God's provision unless there is a need. God is there to provide what we need, but first there has to be a need. The test creates the need, and then the need gives God the opportunity to introduce Himself and fill the need in a fresh, new way.

When the people of Israel trudged through the wilderness for three days and ended up tired and thirsty at Marah, they needed healing. That need allowed God to introduce Himself to them as their healer. God was showing Himself as the remedy, or the cure, to whatever it is that makes us dis-eased. The Israelites had complained, but Moses had cried out. God didn't respond when they complained, but God did reveal Himself when Moses cried out. Complaining doesn't move God, but crying out for His help can.

God's provision for the people of Israel took the form of the tree He showed to Moses, the tree that had been there the entire time. But when you're in a trial, you can't see the tree God provides when you're busy complaining.

The miracle happened when Moses cast the tree into the waters and the waters instantly became sweet. Sometimes God has already provided what you need, but you can't see it until you trust Him, instead of complain to Him. When you cry out to God, trusting that He will heal you of your dis-ease, then He will open your eyes to what is there right in front of you.

Sometime after Brandon and Gina were home and safe, they found out the owner of the backpack with the matches was a man who had died out in the wilderness. His body was found later by a group of searchers, and it wasn't far from the abandoned campsite. Somehow they had not seen the body, but they *had* seen the matches that saved their lives. They realized with a shudder that if the man had not perished and left his belongings, they might not have survived. The loss of his life meant the salvation of theirs.

In the story of Moses and the branch, the tree is like the cross that Jesus died on, with His death meaning new life for us. Through the cross our dis-ease can be mended and repaired. Through the cross the bitter things in life become sweet. Through the cross we can have divine provision for every trial or situation we will ever face because the cross gives us new life through the sacrifice of God's Son.

But it's not enough to know the cross is there. You have to apply the cross to your situation. You have to drag it and throw it into the bitter water that is causing you dis-ease. Remember that tests and challenges are opportunities for God's provision, allowing God to introduce Himself in a fresh, new way into your wilderness, or your bitter place, where He can offer healing.

God lovingly designed our lives so there will be balance. After the bitterness of Marah, God brought His people to Elim, a beautiful oasis providing shade and refreshment. God had already planned for them to come to the place of refreshing—all they needed to do was trust Him. What determines how quickly you move from the testing to the refreshing is the trusting. An awareness of the test and a willful decision to trust means a quicker transition to the oasis and a cool, fresh breeze on your situation.

Don't stay in the wilderness. Hurry to the oasis.

## POINTS TO REMEMBER

- God's people were saved from slavery in Egypt, but when the celebration was over, they went out into the wilderness for a period of wandering.
- God wanted to reveal an important part of His nature, so He healed them at the bitter spring of Marah. To be a healer means to be a fixer, or someone who can cure a disease or injury.
- Every one of us is broken and in need of mending. We are all dis-eased in some way, whether in grief, loss, disappointment, or difficulties of some kind or another.

- God loves us and pledges to keep us from dis-ease. While we may spend time in the wilderness, He will lead us through bad situations and into a bountiful land He's prepared for us.
- This wilderness process takes time. Tests and trials mean God is shaping and molding you for what lies ahead. God allows you to come to places of testing to see if you will trust Him. But just like He takes care of the birds and the flowers, He will certainly take care of you.
- After the bitterness of Marah, God brought His people to a beautiful oasis, a place of refreshment. How quickly you move from testing to refreshing is determined by how quickly you learn to trust God.

## QUESTIONS TO PONDER

1. Have you ever felt like Brandon and Gina? Wandering in a wilderness and hoping for someone to find you and help you out?

2. Do you think of God as a healer of physical disease only? Or do you know Him as a healer of dis-ease? Have you asked Him to fix your own areas of dis-ease, whether it's finances, relationships, work issues, or health problems?

3. Have you ever spent time wandering in the wilderness? Were you aware that it was a wilderness time for you and that you were being shaped and molded by God?

4. How is God taking care of you like He cares for the birds and the flowers?

5. What is an oasis God has provided for you? Have you ever experienced a time of rest and refreshment that seemed like a gift from God?

# CHAPTER 9

# Father God
# (Not the Godfather)

*The question is not "How am I to love God?" but "How am I to let myself be loved by God?" God is looking into the distance for me, trying to find me, and longing to bring me home.*
—HENRI NOUWEN, *THE RETURN OF THE PRODIGAL SON*

T he boy was on the edge of manhood and he was tall, skinny, and perpetually hungry. Even though his mom worked hard to cook three hearty meals a day to keep him full, he still raided the fridge for leftovers whenever he could, and he was always the first one at the dinner table. He couldn't seem to get enough to eat.

Luckily, the boy was part of a big family that loved to cook, and Sunday was his favorite day of the week because everyone got together and loaded the dining table with family recipes.

One Sunday in the springtime, the boy's aunt and uncle

invited him on a road trip to visit some distant family. The trip would take several days there and back, so they planned to leave in the summertime, right after school was out. The boy was excited; he loved his aunt and uncle, and they had always been kind to him, so he knew it was going to be a fun trip. Plus, he looked forward to eating out. Because his parents didn't have much extra money, eating at a restaurant or diner was a rare treat.

Finally, departure day arrived and the boy's aunt and uncle picked him up in their car. It was an older model, a bit worn, but they kept it clean and shiny. The boy hopped in the back seat and off they went. After several hours, the boy was—you guessed it— hungry. He asked if they could stop and get a hamburger. "Of course!" said his aunt.

They found a diner and settled into a shiny red booth. The boy grabbed the menu, his mouth watering as he looked for the biggest burger. "I'll have a triple burger with cheese," he told the server.

"Fries?" she asked.

"Yes. And a strawberry milkshake."

"Whipped cream and a cherry?"

"Yes, *please!*"

Now his mouth was really watering, and he fidgeted with the salt and pepper until his food came. *Bam!* The burger, fries, and shake disappeared within minutes. It all tasted so good.

Back in the car they went, and after a few hundred miles, they stopped at another café in another town for dinner. This time the boy ordered fried chicken, and it really was finger-licking good. His aunt and uncle watched him eat with big smiles.

But by day four, he began to notice something strange. While he always ordered the biggest, heartiest meal on the menu of whatever restaurant they stopped at, his aunt and uncle ordered very little. A cup of soup here, a plate of scrambled eggs there. *Are they on a diet?* he wondered, as he wolfed down yet another chili cheese dog. He knew older people sometimes needed to watch their weight or eat special foods for their health.

All along the way there and back, the aunt and uncle continued to eat like sparrows, ordering small dishes and slowly picking at their food. Sometimes they didn't order anything at all—just a cup of coffee or tea sprinkled with extra sugar. It wasn't until the trip was almost over and they were almost all the way back home that the thought hit him.

*What if they don't have enough money to order what they want? What if they're using all their money to feed* me?

The french fries he was eating no longer tasted quite as good, and he put them down. The boy looked up at his aunt and uncle, who smiled again. They looked a little tired, dark shadows under their eyes. But those eyes were full of love for their nephew, and suddenly he knew it was true. They'd been starving themselves on the trip so he could order whatever he wanted at restaurants and fill himself up.

They didn't have much, but because they loved him, they were giving him whatever they had, and that was much more satisfying to them than a mere sandwich. Their love was extravagant, poured out in the form of juicy burgers and crispy fries. Their generosity and lavish care had a profound impact on him, and as the boy grew into a man, he did what he saw his aunt and uncle do and always gave away more than he should.

This kind of extravagant giving doesn't make a whole lot of sense because it usually can't be reciprocated. Jesus once told a story about a good, good father who was generous like this in a parable called the Prodigal Son, also sometimes called the Lost

Son. It's a powerful story where the heart of the father is on full display with a love so generous, it doesn't make sense.

Jesus told the story to two groups of outsiders. The first group was made up of the hardhearted, judgmental tax collectors and Pharisees. The second group was the sinners.[1] The tax collectors were known to be in cahoots with the government, constantly raising taxes, skimming money off the top, and cheating everyone. The religious leaders were self-righteous hypocrites who liked to point out sin in other people's lives while pretending they were perfect. The sinners were the broken, the outcasts, the folks who couldn't—or didn't want to—obey the complicated system of Jewish laws.

Jesus wanted to teach both groups what made the heart of His Father beat, so of course He told them a story about a father and his two sons. One day the younger son came to his father and said, "Give me my share of the inheritance." What he was asking for wasn't the problem, as he knew he was due to inherit a share of his father's wealth. The problem was that he asked for it early.

In that culture the division of the inheritance only occurred on the death of the father, so this was a sign of deep disrespect. Culturally, he was saying, "Dad, I wish you were dead. I want to live my life as if your values, your presence, and your influence is dead to me." In other words, he wanted to live life on his own terms. He wanted the father's stuff but he didn't want the relationship. He wanted freedom but he didn't want his father.

It would be as if the boy on the road trip with his aunt and uncle sat them down one day along the way and said, "Hey, I see what you're doing here, and I want you to know I appreciate it. But I'm tired of traveling this road with you, so I'd like to have the rest of the food money you have in your pocketbooks, and I'll take it and be on my way. So long!"

That would be foolish, right? He wasn't quite prepared to go out on his own, he didn't really know how to handle money yet, and can you imagine how that would have made his kind aunt and uncle feel?

Can you relate? There are only two ways to live—you can do it your way or the Father's way. And most of us want to do life our own way. "I appreciate you giving me life," the younger son is saying, "but now I'm going to live it on my own terms."

That's what the younger son in the parable did. His father gave him his inheritance, and the son took the money and took off on his own. But here's the thing—doing life your own way and in your own timing will always lead to a dead end. But squandering that money must have been a great feeling. In fact, sin *is* the greatest feeling at first, but it always ends badly. It feels good while you're in it, but if you fast-forward, the end is destruction. "Our desires make us sin," wrote James, the brother of Jesus, "and when sin is finished with us, it leaves us dead."[2]

The difference between our way and the Father's way is the difference between death and life. Jesus explained the end result: "The thief comes only to steal and kill and destroy; I have come that they may have life, and have it to the full."[3]

The younger son's adventure ended abruptly when he found himself without any money and working a menial job. Actually, it was worse than a menial job. It was about the worst job anyone could have. He was out in the fields feeding garbage to a herd of pigs, and since he had absolutely nothing to eat, the garbage the pigs were gobbling down looked like a feast. In that moment, his stomach rumbling while he drooled over what the pigs were eating, his head cleared, and he finally came to his senses.

*My father's workers eat three delicious meals a day. They are much better off than I am. What was I thinking?! I don't want to live like this anymore.*

Although the younger brother had finally come to himself, it had taken a long and painful journey to get there. But somewhere inside he already knew it was all worth it for the lesson he had learned. So he picked himself up, dusted himself off the best he could, and headed for home.

You might be at a similar crossroads right now in your own life, in a field with the pigs and so hungry that garbage looks like a feast to you. Perhaps the thing you said you would never do is what sin has made you do. But whatever led you to this moment of clarity is worth it. Whatever you've had to go through to decide to get up and go back home to your Father is going to be worth it. Get up and go—don't settle into the mud. Don't stay in dysfunction.

While the younger son was limping his way back home, he rehearsed a speech he wanted to give his father. "Father, I've sinned against God, I've sinned before you; I don't deserve to be called your son. Take me on as a hired hand."[4] The words were dramatic, and he hoped his father would respond with forgiveness. He didn't really know what to expect, but he was hoping there would be a place for him at his father's house. He was even willing to slop the pigs, if that's what it took (although I'm sure he was hoping for something a little better than the situation he'd just abandoned).

But as he stumbled on his way home, somehow his father saw him far off in the distance and came running to meet him. "His heart pounding, he ran out, embraced [his son], and kissed him," reads *The Message* version of the Bible. His dad didn't care that his son was covered in filth; he embraced him anyway. And he didn't care about the speech, because he wasn't looking for a big dramatic gesture of repentance. The good father simply loved his son and wanted him back. He cut off the speech, interrupting his son and grabbing him in a big hug. That was all he wanted. The words could wait.

All of us have made mistakes, and so we know exactly how the younger son must have felt. There is fear as we wonder how God is going to respond. *Will He be angry? Will He lose patience with me? Will He give up on me?*

Or worse. *Maybe because of what I've done, I've disqualified myself and will no longer be eligible for God's love. It's all over for me because I've messed up too bad.*

The younger son was coming back knowing he'd messed up, knowing he'd not fit to take his place as son again, so he hoped to at least return in a lowly servant's role. He planned to work hard, say and do the right things, and maybe get back into the graces of his father at some far-off point in the future. It was going to be a lot of work, if it was even possible.

So the father's response was more than surprising. He came running to meet his son, not seeming to care that he was coming back without the money, coming back ceremonially unclean (after working with pigs), and coming back in disgrace. All the father wanted was to have his son back. That's all he cared about.

And it was a shock to the younger son. He couldn't quite wrap his mind around it. Not only was his father accepting him back as his son, but he was calling for food, and guests, and a party. He met him with a ring and a robe—exactly how God meets us when we turn back and seek Him out. We're broken and we've failed after trying life our own way, and God wants us back. It's hard to believe, and yet it's true.

But what about the son who stayed? Jesus said the older son was out in the field working when all this was going on, and, when the day's work was done, he started home for dinner. He must have been tired and hungry. But as he got close to the house, instead of smelling dinner he heard loud music and saw dancing.

"What's going on?" he demanded of one of his father's servants.

"Your brother came home," said the servant. "Your father has ordered a feast . . . because he has him home safe and sound."

The older brother's response was completely different from the father's. Instead of joy, he reacted with anger and refused to join the party. When his father tried to talk to him, he became enraged. "Look! All these years I've been slaving for you and never disobeyed your orders. Yet you never gave me even a young goat so I could celebrate with my friends. But when this son of yours who has squandered your property with prostitutes comes home, you kill the fattened calf for him!"

"Son, [you don't understand,]" said the good father. "you are always with me, and everything I have is yours. But we had to celebrate and be glad, because this brother of yours was dead and is alive again; he was lost and is found."[5]

The son who stayed was as disrespectful as the son who left; he just handled his disrespect differently. But their hearts were the same—both sons wanted their father's stuff, instead of really wanting the father.

One of the reasons Jesus told this parable is because all of us fit into one of these two categories. Either we left the Father's care and decided to try and do it our own way, or we stayed, but for the wrong reasons.

But before you exhale and think, *Thank God I'm not like that fool of a younger brother,* stop a minute. Is it possible you have the spirit of the elder brother? Because sometimes this spirit creeps into the church, and when a broken, despairing person comes through the doors, there is judgment and condemnation rather than love and acceptance.

People come back to the church after a long time away, or come into the church for the first time, and they brace themselves for condemnation. If we can meet them figuratively with a party, a ring, and a robe, everything will change. If we can open our hearts and embrace those who are struggling, we will display the love of the good father Jesus described in His story. Jesus told the story to show us how to welcome in the broken and the hurting with the love of the Father.

While the younger brother was clearly wrong, the elder brother was too. Lasting change comes from the loving embrace of the Father, which resets the heart of the son. If the broken, struggling heart isn't reset by the love of the Father, the change won't last, or even come in the first place.

Do you fit into one of these two categories: the younger brother who rebels or the elder brother who judges?

Here are a few signs of an elder-brother spirit:

- Anger, superiority, and self-righteousness: *The older brother became angry and refused to go in . . .*
- Words dripping with bitterness and resentment: *"Have you ever thrown a party for me and my friends?"*
- Believing if you do all the right things, then life will be good and everything will work out right for you: *"Look how many ways I've stayed here serving you!"*

In other words, the only reason the elder brother was obedient and hard working is because of what he wanted to get during his brother's absence—his father's favor and his father's wealth. He wanted whatever was left for himself. His motivation slipped out when he said, "I've been slaving for you." The word *slave* meant he felt as if he was being forced to work hard, instead of desiring to do it. A slave works out of fear, not out of love, admiration, or joy. So even though the elder brother did all the right things, he did it for the wrong reasons.

The great preacher Charles Spurgeon told a story about a gardener who worked hard in his garden and grew a beautiful bunch of carrots. He pulled them out of the soil and took them to the king as a gift. "My lord," he said, holding up a carrot, "this is the greatest carrot I've ever grown or ever will grow. Therefore I want to present it to you as a token of my love for you!"

The king was touched and wanted to reward the man. The best gift he could think of was a plot of land so the man could grow an even bigger garden and thus continue to bless the kingdom.

A courtier who witnessed the exchange decided to give a gift of his own. The next day he brought a beautiful horse to the court and presented it to the king, hoping for a reward that matched his costly gift. Surely a highly bred and trained horse would be worth far more than a bunch of vegetables.

Surprise! The king awarded the man nothing, simply accepting the gift with a thank-you. When the courtier looked disappointed, the king explained: "The gardener gave me the carrots, but you have given *yourself* the horse. You gave not for love of me, but for love of yourself, in the hope of a reward."

In the end, elder brothers may do the right thing but for the wrong reasons. Our good, good Father God doesn't want us to do anything because we *have* to. He wants us to do the right thing because we love Him as He loves us. The elder brother thinks that if he does all the right things, and does them perfectly, then his father will love him. And so many of us try to approach God the same way. But you don't have to. Since Jesus did all the work, you don't have to do anything for Him to love you.

The word *prodigal* in this story is often used to refer to the son who took his inheritance and left. But that is not the case. The word *prodigal* does not mean "wayward" or "rebellious." Instead, it means "recklessly extravagant, lavish, to give profusely."

Each brother had his own perspective on life and both had failed. Yet the father still lavished his love on them, reaching out and inviting both the younger and the older brothers into relationship and the abundance of his love.

The word *prodigal* is not only a description of the younger son; it describes the father. The extravagant love of the father is what Jesus wants us to see. The father doesn't point out the sins and shortcomings of the sons.

Instead, he lavishes them with his love. He gives his love to his children in profusion, and that's the way our good, good Father is with us. His love is lavish without end.

## POINTS TO REMEMBER

- Extravagant giving, where you give generously to someone who can't pay you back, is almost always a surprise. It doesn't make sense to most people.
- The story of the prodigal son is about a good father who demonstrated an extravagant love that reflects the heart of God.
- Jesus told the story to two groups of people, both outcasts in the community. The story showed there are two ways to live—you can do life your way, or the Father's way.

- The younger son took his inheritance and squandered it, then wanted to come home. You might be in a similar situation and need to go home to your Father. Do it now—don't settle into dysfunction.
- The returning son was greeted with joy by the father. He was needlessly afraid of the father's response and felt like he was no longer eligible for his father's love.
- The older son reacted negatively with judgment and resentment. He was as disrespectful as the younger son; he just handled his disrespect differently.
- All of us have either the rebellious spirit of the younger brother or the judgmental spirit of the older brother. Yet, the Father loved them both. He invited them both into relationship and the abundance of His love.

## QUESTIONS TO PONDER

1. When you were a kid, did you have a big appetite, like the boy in the story? What was your favorite food to indulge in?
2. In the story of the prodigal son, do you relate more to the younger son (in reckless rebellion) or the older son (in arrogant judgment)?
3. When you return to God the Father after a time away from Him, do you always expect to be greeted with joy? Or do you expect Him to respond with a refusal to love you? Or a blast of angry judgment?
4. Why do you think the older son was so angry and bitter at his father's acceptance of the younger brother? What was bothering him?

5. Have you ever felt that your past actions or mistakes have disqualified you for the Father's love? How did you get past that feeling of rejection and defeat and embrace God's love?

6. Were you surprised by the meaning of the word *prodigal*? Does that change the emphasis of the story for you? Does it change your understanding of who God is?

# CHAPTER 10

# More Than Enough

*The hunger for love is much more difficult to*
*remove than the hunger for bread.*
—Mother Teresa

D o you remember the last time you were hungry? I'm talking really, really hungry. Your stomach empty. Your innards
growling. Or, as a friend used to say, "It feels like my stomach is
eating itself."

It's an uncomfortable feeling to say the least. When you're hungry or thirsty, it's hard to think about anything else except finding
some food to fill your stomach or water to quench your thirst. Both
are powerful, driving forces, and the hungrier or thirstier you get,
the stronger the compulsion to eat or drink something, anything,
to make it stop.

While we're all familiar with that feeling, there are some
people who feel that craving twenty-four hours a day. It's called

Prader-Willi syndrome, a genetic disease that causes chronic feelings of insatiable hunger. This rare condition affects about one in every twelve to fifteen thousand people. Prader-Willi also causes other problems, such as learning issues, but for sufferers and their families the appetite issues are the main concern. Finding and consuming food is the number one priority. Kate Kane, who has Prader-Willi syndrome, described it like this: "I could eat until I die, basically."[1]

People with Prader-Willi syndrome never feel full or satisfied, even after a meal. Kane will "do literally anything for food." Sufferers can get in trouble at school or lose relationships and jobs, and some have been arrested for shoplifting and consuming food items. Families are forced to lock up kitchen cabinets, pantries, and refrigerators and freezers to prevent midnight food raids.

"Her hunger gets in the way of everything," said Kate's father. It's hard for Prader-Willi sufferers to have a happy life when they can never get enough food, no matter how much they eat. So far, scientists have no cure for the condition. Left untreated, Kate and others with the condition typically end up grossly obese and at risk for diabetes and cardiovascular problems.

Think about it—no matter how many hamburgers you eat, how much pasta you consume, how many sandwiches you have, or how many bowls of cereal you slurp down in the morning, you can never fill yourself up. Your cravings are in charge, not you. You're obsessed with food. You're empty and looking to be filled every single second of every day, all year long. For your entire life.

While Prader-Willi syndrome is an extreme example of never feeling you have enough food to feel full and satisfied, there are many other cravings that can take over your life. Some people struggle with strong and persistent cravings for sex, drugs, or alcohol. Horror writer Stephen King once told the story of fighting his alcohol cravings, explaining how he couldn't sleep if he knew there was any alcohol in the house. He would lie in his bed, feeling like the bottle was calling to him. Before he could go to sleep, he'd have to get out of bed, go to the kitchen, and pour the wine or beer down the sink. Then and only then could he find rest.

Other people fight their own obsessions with shopping, gambling, or pornography. Even seemingly innocuous pleasures such as coffee, diet soda, movie theater popcorn, or even exercise can become harsh taskmasters when a person can't seem to stop. It's never a good feeling to be in perpetual need of more, more, more.

Coffee is a common addiction, and specialty coffee shops know that the more caffeine they infuse into their products, the more customers will crave them. There are quizzes scattered around the Internet that will tell you if you're addicted to Starbucks or not. Hint: you might be in trouble if the barista knows you and your order by name.

The pursuit of wealth and worldly success is another appetite that is hard to tame. So often people spend much of their lives going after things instead of going after God. Then they get to the end of their lives and realize that everything without Him is really nothing. The food pantry is bare, the fancy paper coffee cup is empty, but the desire for more is still there.

People living during the time of Jesus had all the common cravings we have, although they might have been popping dried dates or figs instead of movie theater popcorn. They were going about their lives, trying to make themselves feel better and pursuing whatever seemed to satisfy their longings. Just like us, they could never get enough to really be happy.

Since He was fully God and fully human, Jesus felt these cravings too. He understood extreme hunger and thirst, and there was a day when He showed up at a well in the region of Samaria, both hungry and thirsty. It was the noon hour, and he sat, tired and waiting, as a woman arrived to draw water.

"Would you give me a drink of water?" He asked politely.

The Samaritan woman, taken aback, asked, "How come you, a Jew, are asking me, a Samaritan woman, for a drink?" In those days Jewish people wouldn't be caught dead talking to Samaritan people. Two thousand years ago, people also struggled with categorizing others and giving in to their biases and prejudices. Racism and other judgmental isms were alive and well in the ancient world.

Ten kinds of prejudice have been identified:

- Racial
- Sexual
- Chronological (age-ism)
- Geographical
- Educational
- Financial
- Physical
- Denominational
- Ministerial
- Doctrinal

All these prejudices are bad, but what is even worse is that they all have oozed their way into the church. In today's world, racism is currently one of the most difficult and painful challenges we face. How can we overcome it? It's significant to note that when you put a big G (for God) in front of the word "race," you get "Grace." Grace is bigger than race.

There is no prejudice in Christ, and for certain there is no racial prejudice in Christ. The Jesus many of us think we know is a Jesus of our own making. We have constructed an image of Him from various experiences, failures, and victories. The problem is that the Jesus we have constructed is different from the Jesus who really existed. We'll never penetrate the world with the good news until the good news first penetrates the world between our ears.

So regardless of what the Jews thought of the Samaritans, Jesus brought a message of grace and went after the woman at the well like the Good Shepherd goes after the lost sheep. And not only did Jesus go after her, but He also went ahead of her, because He got to the well before she did. He was waiting on her to get there, and He couldn't wait to talk to her.

Not only was it unusual for a Jewish person to be talking to a Samaritan, but talking to a woman in public was also frowned on. Yet Jesus did what He always did by rising above the stereotypes and demonstrating what Paul would later say in Galatians—in Christ there is no Jew or Greek, slave or free, male or female.

Jesus answered the woman with a hint of His identity, and a significant but mysterious promise. "If you knew the generosity of God and who I am, you would be asking *me* for a drink, and I would give you fresh, living water."

The woman was intrigued. "Sir, you don't even have a bucket to draw with, and this well is deep. So how are you going to get this 'living water'? Are you a better man than our ancestor Jacob, who dug this well and drank from it, he and his sons and livestock, and passed it down to us?" The Samaritans were an offshoot of the Jewish religion. They believed in Mosaic law, so the woman challenged Jesus to explain who He was and what He was all about. She was wondering if she'd missed something. Was this strange man teaching something more important than the law?

Then Jesus explained something incredible. The living water? It's an unconditional gift. It doesn't have to be earned. "Everyone who drinks this water will get thirsty again and again. Anyone who drinks the water I give will never thirst—not ever. The water I give will be an artesian spring within, gushing fountains of endless life."

Thirsty and yearning for this living water, the woman believed what Jesus said and asked him for something that would change her life. "Sir, give me this water so I won't ever get thirsty, won't ever have to come back to this well again!"[2]

As their conversation continued, her checkered past came to light (five husbands and currently living with a man she was not married to, and Jesus knew all this and called her out on it). Yet even then, Jesus continued the discussion with her. There was no condemnation from Him as He responded to her hunger for the truth.

The thirsty woman daring to approach Jesus is a picture of so many of us, yearning for fulfillment. She'd been looking for fulfillment everywhere, except from the one true, living God. The prophet Jeremiah shared God's view on this: "My people have committed two sins: They have forsaken me, the spring of living water, and have dug their own cisterns, broken cisterns that cannot hold water."[3]

It's a sorrowful and fruitless way to live when you're pursuing happiness and fulfillment from activities, people, and material goods that can never fulfill you. Countless celebrities, successful businesspeople, and incredibly creative artists and musicians have spent their lives climbing the ladder of success, only to get to the top and find out their ladders are propped up against the wrong wall.

Michael Jackson's story is one of those tales. He seemed to have it all—one of the greatest and most talented entertainers of all time—yet he was a man who struggled in so many areas and could never seem to find contentment. He couldn't seem to find rest, and his quest for peaceful sleep is what finally finished him off when he overdosed on a powerful sedative.

In contrast, a young and talented woman named Megan Boudreaux learned early on that there was more to life than money and fame. Megan was a bright young college student who majored in political science, graduated, and found a good job in the health industry, and was ready to take almost any challenge that came her way. Her job took her on a trip to Haiti, and one afternoon before she left to fly home, she took a walk on a grassy hill. There she met a little girl with ragged clothes. The girl was throwing rocks at birds, hoping to knock one down so she could eat it. She appeared to be starving.

Megan left but never forgot the little girl, and before long she quit her job, sold everything she had, and moved to Haiti. She had nothing waiting—no house, job, or plan. She found the little girl, discovered she was an orphan, adopted her, and then started a school for children at risk. Today Megan runs a thriving nonprofit called Respire Haiti, with a school for five hundred children, a health clinic, a café, and a recycling center. She is remaking the community one child at a time. She could probably have made more money and had a bigger, more comfortable house if she'd stayed at her job in the States, but guess what? Megan sleeps well in the messiness and challenges of living in Haiti, knowing she's helping the boys and girls of her community, and their families, get to know a God who cares about each and every one of them.

As the conversation between Jesus and the woman at the well

began to wind down, He made a stunning revelation. This piece of information was something He had not yet told anyone else. And it turned out to be the news flash of the year!

It all started when the woman said, "I do know that the Messiah is coming. When he arrives, we'll get the whole story."

"I am he," said Jesus. "You don't have to wait any longer or look any further."[4]

The Samaritan woman was the first person Jesus revealed His true identity to, and it was such a surprise. There was no audience, just a quiet conversation between Jesus and an outcast over a drink of water. Jesus met her where she was, at her point of need, and revealed His true identity based on her need. He asked for a drink of water, but He gave her so much more in return—the truth of who He was, the forgiveness of her past, the promise of eternal life, and hope for the future. With that, the private conversation was over because she was so excited that she *ran* to tell everyone in town. They listened, and many believed. They begged Jesus to stay and tell them more.

The unlikely woman looking for love in all the wrong places became the first evangelist in the New Testament. She almost seemed to get who Jesus was and what He was on earth to do better than His disciples did. It's a compelling contrast—while they were in town purchasing food (and not making any converts, by the way), she was being fed by Jesus, and soon to be on her way to helping transform her city with the good news of the Messiah.

Whenever Jesus came along with the messages of living water, the bread of life, and grace, most people sat up and listened. Are you listening to the One who can give you the bread of life and the living water you crave? Are you ready to turn away from the hollow offerings of the world to something much, much better?

When you feel overwhelmed with hunger and thirst for things you know are not healthy or good for you, Jesus will be enough because He can fill and satisfy those longings with living water. Jesus is like the ultimate barista who knows you and knows your order and your unhealthy dependence on coffee, and yet He still loves you, cares for you, and yearns to make you free. No cup of coffee is going to fill that emptiness in your soul. It will never be enough.

Through Jesus, you have the ultimate victory over behaviors, attitudes, addictions, and sins that would hold you down, bind you, and keep you from moving forward in your life. No more permanent emptiness, and no more unquenchable longing for satisfaction.

God offers you love and grace, and He is enough.

## POINTS TO REMEMBER

- Two thousand years ago, people struggled with the same prejudices we do: racial, sexual, chronological (age-ism), geographical, educational, financial, physical, denominational, ministerial, doctrinal.
- There is no prejudice in Christ.
- The woman at the well is a picture of so many of us, yearning for fulfillment. It's a sorrowful and fruitless way to live when you're pursuing happiness and fulfillment from activities, people, and material goods that can never fulfill you.
- When you feel overwhelmed with hunger and thirst for things you know are not healthy or good for you, Jesus will be enough because He can fill and satisfy those longings with living water.

- Through Jesus, you have the ultimate victory over behaviors, attitudes, addictions, and sins that would hold you down, bind you, and keep you from moving forward in your life.

## QUESTIONS TO PONDER

1. Think about a craving you've struggled with. It could be anything from a taste for a particular brand of chocolate-chip cookie to something much more serious.
2. How have you gained victory over this craving? Or at least kept it under control?
3. If you haven't yet gained victory, have you invited Jesus into the struggle? And have you done this consistently?
4. Could your craving be related to something deeper? Like the women at the well, many of us are yearning for happiness and fulfillment but not looking in the right place.
5. How can you confront this craving today after taking a fresh look at Jesus' words to the Samaritan woman? Write down a prayer to the Lord Jesus and ask Him to fill your thirst with His living water, using some of the words and ideas from the passage in John 4:1–42.

# CHAPTER 11

# Simple

*If you can't explain it simply, you don't understand it well enough.*
—ALBERT EINSTEIN

To call something simple means it is straightforward, easily understood, and easily done. But even when something or someone is described as simple, there's more going on under the surface than can be seen at first glance. Take Jacob Barnett, for example.

At the age of two, Jacob was diagnosed with moderate to severe autism. He seemed to be developing at a normal rate and then everything changed. Like other autistic kids, Jacob unplugged from the world of human interaction, stopped eye contact, and lost all communication skills. He couldn't even say "Mommy" anymore.[1] His doctor warned his worried mom that he would probably never be able to read, tie his shoes, or talk.

As a treatment plan for his desperate mother, the professionals suggested intensive therapy and special education. His mom tried to follow the plan, but Jacob got worse, withdrawing further into himself. She discovered clues to the boy locked inside—he could create a detailed, perfect map of a place he had visited by arranging hundreds of Q-tips on the kitchen floor. When he was three, he suddenly spoke four languages and seemed to understand the concepts of physics.

His mother had that mama-bear kind of love. She watched and studied her child on her own, and somehow she saw potential where the professional medical practitioners and educators did not. She knew there was something inside Jacob that needed to be unlocked, and she searched hard for the key.

Finally, in desperation she decided to change the treatment plan and take over Jacob's education for herself, homeschooling him and allowing him to study what he wanted and at his own pace. She simplified everything—the treatment plan, the expectations, and the pace. Then something strange happened. Jacob's own pace turned out to be something no one anticipated, and when he was eight years old, he started college courses in physics.

Now eighteen years old, Jacob's IQ has been measured at 170 (higher than Einstein's), and he is working on a new theory of relativity. Some say he's on the fast track to a Nobel Prize. It's likely that if he continues on the path of higher learning and research, someday his intellect and curiosity may advance our understanding of the universe in significant ways.

Was Jacob simple? According to his doctors and teachers, yes, he was.

But is Jacob incredibly intelligent, unique, and innovative? Yes! He experiences the world differently than the rest of us.

Our God is like that too. Simple.

As I've traveled the world, I have seen and experienced many phases and aspects of our Christian faith, and I've finally realized this—in many ways we have made God far too complicated. I know people who are so deep and so dedicated to showing off their knowledge that they act like they've just teleported down from the throne of God. But the problem is they are so deep and complicated, no one understands them at all.

When you spend time in God's Word, what you find is that God and His Son, Jesus, are not that complicated at all. God wants to make it easy for us, as Jacob's mom did for him. There's no jumping through hoops, no impossible-to-reach goals, no report card to slap us in the face with. Part of the reason the Pharisees and Sadducees, the religious leaders in the time of Jesus, had such a big problem with Him is because He did not uphold all their complicated laws.

This is why God has never been about religion. Instead, the heart of God is about loving relationship. Religions are based on rules, but relationships are so much simpler. Because our God is simple, a relationship with Him boils down to three things: belief, love, and service.

First, you have to believe. To believe something, you have to accept it as true, correct, or real. You don't have to test it, prove it, or explain it. You don't have to debate it, defend it, or advertise it. You don't even have to fully understand it. You just have to accept it as true.

In the book of Acts is a story about the simple act of believing in God. The apostle Paul and his friend Silas had accidentally enraged a crowd in the city of Philippi. The angry citizens attacked the two men and dragged them before the local magistrate, who ordered them to be stripped and beaten. Next they were put into an inner cell with their feet fastened into stocks. The jailer was personally warned to keep a close eye on the two new prisoners.

Paul and Silas must have been in intense pain from the brutal treatment, and they were still awake at midnight, praying and singing songs to the Lord with the other prisoners listening. Those prisoners were having some church in that tiny, dark jail! All of a sudden, a powerful earthquake struck, rocking the jail to its foundations. The earthquake caused enough damage to break open the jail doors and cause the prisoners' chains to break off.

When the jailer rushed in and saw the cell doors open, he drew his sword and was about to kill himself. Knowing the brutality of his Roman overlords, he'd decided to beat them to the punch and so avoid a torturous death. But Paul, a man of grace and peace, saw what he was about to do and quickly shouted, "Don't harm yourself. We are all here!"

The jailer put down his sword, knowing these men were different somehow. He fell trembling before Paul and Silas. "Sirs, what must I do to be saved?"

The answer was simple. "Believe in the Lord Jesus, and you will be saved." That was it—all the jailer had to do was believe. He spent the rest of the night taking care of these two prisoners who had become his new mentors, and they shared the good news of the Lord Jesus Christ with him and his family. Then, "he was filled with joy because he had come to believe in God—he and his whole household."[2]

Here are the things he *didn't* have to do to be saved:

- Take a class or earn a degree
- Convert to an established religion
- Keep any laws

- Dress a certain way
- Talk a certain way
- Look a certain way
- Clean up his life
- Free himself from his addictions
- Apologize to anyone
- Seek permission from anyone
- Be approved in advance

All the jailer did was ask a simple question with a simple answer. Then all he had to do was believe, because belief is a function of your heart, not your behavior or intellect. "If you declare with your mouth, 'Jesus is Lord,' and believe in your heart that God raised him from the dead, you will be saved," wrote Paul in the book of Romans.[3] It's simple—*believing* is the way you can have a relationship with Jesus.

The space program in our country, also called NASA, is something that takes a whole lot of belief. Before we put a human into space or asked our astronauts to walk on the moon, there were heated debates in many circles about whether it was at all possible. Even after we accomplished this incredible feat multiple times, with eyewitness testimony from the Mercury 7 astronauts along with detailed documentation to prove we did in fact put a man on the moon, there were still plenty of naysayers who didn't believe it happened. Folks had seen it with their own eyes on television, but for some reason they couldn't seem to accept it as true. They thought it was all fake. For some people, the idea of a man on the moon was too strange, too foreign, and too fantastical to believe.

Scott Parazynski is a noted astronaut who flew on the space shuttle five times and helped to build the International Space

Station. In order to climb into a space suit, he first had to believe he could fly all the way from Earth into space. Before he could fly, he had to believe it could happen.

One evening he took his little boy, Luke, out into the backyard to show him the space station. When it flies overhead, it can easily be seen with the naked eye as the brightest man-made object gliding smoothly across the sky.

Scott and Luke stood together, looking up and waiting, until they spotted it.

"Whoa! You're going up there?!" Luke asked in wonderment.

"Yep," said his dad. "I've been up there once already to help get it started, and now one final trip to finish my part of the job."[4]

It was incredibly hard for Luke to imagine that his dad, who was standing right there beside him, would soon be up in space inside that little dot of light moving across the night sky. But since he knew and trusted his dad, he believed him.

Abraham once had a moment like that. God took him outside to his backyard and said, "Look up at the sky and count the stars—if indeed you can count them." Then came a promise straight from the mouth of God: "So shall your offspring be."[5]

Did Abraham scoff, harden his heart, or turn away in disbelief? He could have. He could have demanded God share His plans with him, because how on earth was he going to have that many descendants when his wife was barren and they didn't even have any children? Not to mention, they were both advanced in years with zero chance of getting pregnant. He could have laughed. Or cried. But he didn't do any of those things.

Instead, Genesis 15:6 says, "[Abraham] believed the LORD, and he [the Lord] credited it to him as righteousness." God made a promise to Abraham, and Abraham simply believed. Abraham didn't have to work for his salvation; all he did was trust God and God credited him with righteousness. *Credited* is a banking term, meaning God deposited righteousness into Abraham's account. What made Abraham right with God was not something he earned or worked for; he believed God in spite of the facts and against all hope. Belief is the first step.

Second, to have a relationship with God you need His love. Before you can love God or love others, you have to receive the love of the Father. "We love because he first loved us," wrote Jesus' best friend, the beloved disciple John.[6] God loved us first, and this enables us to love Him back so we can live our lives empowered by His love, not striving for His love.

Remember the Broadway show, and later a feature film, called *Annie*? A houseful of orphans suffered under a wicked, alcoholic housemother named Miss Hannigan, and each girl longed to be lifted up and out of this terrible situation. The orphans hoped and dreamed about escaping, and everything they did was in hope of being loved and chosen for adoption by a real, live, loving, and caring family. Miss Hannigan took full advantage of the orphans and made them cook and clean so she could live like a princess with a houseful of slaves.

Are we really that different? Many of us are already in the family of God, and we have an orphan mentality, convinced we have to do the right things in order to be loved by our Father. But God's love is without conditions. He doesn't ask for anything from us in order to love us.

Jesus gave His life for you before you were even born. "You see, at just the right time, when we were still powerless, Christ died for the ungodly. . . . God demonstrates his own love for us in this: While we were still sinners, Christ died for us."[7] So it doesn't matter what you ever do wrong or right, you will always be completely and unconditionally loved by Him. You didn't do anything to earn His love, which also means you can't do anything to lose His love.

You're not loved because of anything you could ever do; you are loved because you are His child. When my kids were born, they didn't have to do anything to earn my love. I loved them because they are my kids, and I loved them before they ever took a breath of air on this earth. There was nothing my son or my daughter had to do for me to love them. When they were born they received my love. Simple.

Finally, after believing God and receiving his love, you need to love and serve others. "Love each other as I have loved you," said Jesus.[8] Loving others is a new command from Jesus, because "by this everyone will know that you are my disciples, if you love one another."[9]

Sometimes loving others is easier said than done. So often we want to love others based on how we feel or how they love us, but that's not the command. The command is to love, and with that comes service. Jesus modeled this in John 13 when He took the place of a lowly servant and got up from dinner, knelt down, and washed the feet of His disciples. After tenderly drying their feet, He taught them why He'd done it.

During this last meal of His life, Jesus showed us how to live our lives—as servants. "Do you understand what I have done for you? . . . You call me 'Teacher' and 'Lord,' and rightly so, for that is what I am. Now that I, your Lord and Teacher, have washed your feet, you also should wash one another's feet. I have set you an example that you should do as I have done for you. . . . Now that you know these things, you will be blessed if you do them."[10]

Serving is not a low, inconsequential position. Sometimes

people don't like to serve because they think it's beneath them. But serving takes strength, along with the security of knowing who you are. When you believe God and you know and accept His love for you, you know who you are and you can serve. There's an old proverb that says, "The fuller the ear of corn, the lower it bends." Jesus bent down to serve His disciples and to show us how to live. When you know who you are and what you have, you serve.

A man named Henri Nouwen is a powerful example of someone who believed, received God's love, and then loved and served others. A priest, theologian, and writer, Henri was also a noted and beloved professor at Yale, Harvard, and Notre Dame. His books were, and still are, read by millions. But at the height of his career, Henri left what he was doing and went to work at a facility for mentally and physically handicapped people. He didn't go there to teach them or write for them or supervise them; he went there to serve.

Henri served with his own hands in full humility, without trying to avoid any difficult, painful, or trying task in caring for those who couldn't care for themselves. He devoted himself to serving those whose disabilities "placed them on the margin of society."[11] He walked side by side with them, wiped their mouths, and changed their diapers.

"In their poverty, the mentally handicapped reveal God to us and hold us close to the gospel," explained Nouwen. He admitted the work could be draining, both physically and emotionally exhausting. Yet, it was important work because caring for others is a reflection of God's care for us. Nouwen loved the people he was serving because he understood and accepted God's love for him.

"Compassion asks us to go where it hurts, to enter into the places of pain, to share in brokenness, fear, confusion, and anguish," wrote Nouwen. "Compassion challenges us to cry out with those in misery, to mourn with those who are lonely, to weep with those in tears. Compassion requires us to be weak with the weak, vulnerable with the vulnerable, and powerless with the powerless. Compassion means full immersion in the condition of being human."

That full immersion in the condition of being human is an elegant way of describing what it means to have a relationship. It means getting close to people, knowing them, believing them, accepting them, loving and being loved by them, and serving them.

God wants us close to Him, so He doesn't make it complicated to learn how to get close to Him. Belief, love, and service. It's that simple.

## POINTS TO REMEMBER

- When you spend time in God's Word, what you find is that God and His Son, Jesus, are not that complicated at all.
- God wants to make it easy for us. There's no jumping through hoops, no impossible-to-reach goals, no report card to slap us in the face with.
- God has never been about religion. Instead the heart of God is about relationship.
- Relationships mean getting close to people, knowing them, believing them, accepting them, loving and being loved by them, and serving them.
- To have a relationship with God, you have to believe. Second, to have a relationship with God you need His love. Finally, after believing God and receiving His love, you need to love and serve others.

- You're not loved because of anything you could ever do; you are loved because you are His child.

## QUESTIONS TO PONDER

1. Have you ever felt like knowing God can be complicated? Do you know someone who feels that way?
2. What are some ways that people make knowing and following God complicated and difficult?
3. Were you brought up to feel like God is more about religion and rules, or relationship? How did this impact your faith journey for better or for worse?
4. Sometimes people feel like they need to earn God's love. What are some things people do to try to earn points with God?
5. What's the first thing you need to do to accept Jesus? (Hint: Abraham did this and it was credited to him as righteousness.)
6. After believing in God comes service. How can you show God you love Him by serving someone else today?

# CHAPTER 12

# No Mountain High Enough

*The mountain is tough. No matter how meticulous you
may be, it is a dangerous place. Be humble.*
—KILIAN JORNET, EXTREME RUNNER AND MOUNTAIN CLIMBER

For people who love a physical challenge, climbing Mount
Everest is the ultimate adventure. At 29,029 feet high, and
with atmospheric pressure at the top cutting the available oxygen
to one-third of that at sea level, it's a dangerous place.

In reality, the top of Everest is a place not meant for humans to
inhabit for more than a few minutes. Plus there is the potential for
suffering through two-hundred-mile-per-hour winds, avalanches,
falling rocks, whiteouts, frostbite, altitude sickness, crevasse falls,
witnessing the accidental deaths of other climbers, or experiencing
sudden death yourself.

So why on earth do people attempt Everest? When you ask
these extreme climbers why they do what they do, the most

common answer is, "Because it's there." But if you dig deeper, it comes down to a love for the outdoors, a love for the common bond they feel with the community of climbers and mountaineers, and a love for the mountaintop accomplishment. Climbers love what they do, and that's why it doesn't always make sense to others. But these explorers are a tribe, and the members of that tribe understand one another, encourage one another, support one another, and love one another. They need help from their tribe to be safe so they can do what they love to do.

Recently, an ultra marathoner named Kilian Jornet climbed Mount Everest in a record-breaking twenty-six hours without the use of oxygen or fixed ropes. It was an unprecedented feat. Usually it takes months of effort as wishful climbers hike up and down the mountain, striving to acclimate their bodies to the punishing high altitudes. But Jornet's training regimen is relentless; he trains hard every day, all year long, year after year. Even this extreme athlete respects the dangers of Everest, and in his blog he explains how he plans carefully and takes every precaution possible in order to stay safe:

> First and foremost, bear in mind that ours is a sport performed in a natural environment that we do not control. So learn to know the mountain and learn how to interact with it. Take all the safety measures necessary, watch the weather forecast, do not go out into the mountains alone, trust specialists, etc. I was born and raised there, and have spent many years out in the mountains as part of my daily routine. That is why I probably have more experience in some circumstances. However, I will never be negligent when it comes to safety measures or protection. The mountain is tough. No matter how meticulous you may be, it is a dangerous place. Be humble in the mountains . . . [1]

The reality is many climbers make an attempt at the summit, but not everyone makes it—the success rate is only about one in three. Every year an average of five climbers die during the Everest climbing season, and some years there are more. Yet, every year hundreds of people spend thousands of dollars and hours preparing to climb Everest. Wannabe climbers buy books, research online, watch videos, talk to experts, and spend a great deal of money to sign on with experienced expedition companies. Always, because of the known dangers, the aspiring Everest climber's key question is this: *What do I need to do to be safe?* The answer is to learn and get help and support from your tribe.

While the question of how to stay safe is important for a mountain climber, it's a question we all ask ourselves sooner or later, especially in regard to life after death. If you believe that humans are spiritual beings and that there is some sort of afterlife, sooner or later you'll tangle with this same key question: *What do I need to do to be safe?* Many people with different motivations asked Jesus this question face-to-face, and their stories are recorded in the Bible.

On one occasion, Jesus and His disciples were making their way to Jerusalem and were somewhere near the village of Bethany, where his close friends Mary, Martha, and Lazarus lived. On this particular day, while Jesus was teaching, a so-called expert in the law stood up to test Jesus, and he raised this exact question: "Teacher, . . . what must I do to inherit eternal life?"

In other words, what do I need to do to be saved?

"What is written in the law?" Jesus asked in response. "How do *you* read it?"[2]

It's important to note that the question about how to be saved is coming from a noted teacher who is already part of the established religion. He was part of the status quo, but he still had the same question: How do I stay safe when this life is over? How can I be saved from death and judgment?

After some back and forth with the teacher, Jesus told a story. "A certain man went down from Jerusalem to Jericho, and fell among thieves, who stripped him of his clothing, wounded him, and departed, leaving him half dead."[3] Notice Jesus didn't give the man a name because this man represents every single one of us. He is every man and every woman.

The man was walking the road from the holy city of Jerusalem, situated at 2,500 feet above sea level, down to Jericho, "the Fallen City," at 1,300 feet below sea level. That meant a 3,600-foot drop in elevation in a short, twenty-mile journey. But in that short journey, things changed forever for the man as he went from being on top to being on the bottom. His life journey suddenly changed, as it can for any one of us. A phone call, an e-mail, a meeting—or an accident or a medical or relational crisis—we all know how everything can change for us in a few seconds. Storms can roll in seemingly from nowhere.

When the man going down to Jericho fell, Jesus said he fell among thieves. The moment he fell, his enemies were there, ready to take advantage and prey on him in the most vicious way. Where were his friends? Where were the helpful bystanders? For some reason, he was left to suffer this attack alone.

You might have experienced this part of the story too. When difficulties arise, friends can be unaware of what you're going through, or even turn or fade away, and you're left to go through the situation alone. Sometimes the emotional pain of being left all by yourself in a difficult situation is worse than the pain of the actual situation. It hurts when so-called friends leave you at your lowest point, because that's the kind of behavior you expect from your enemies, not your friends. When you need help, whatever your storm or struggle is, and you don't get it—that's devastating. Isolation in difficult situations is not only painful, it's dangerous. Climbers on Everest who become isolated risk dying alone. The man in Jesus' story faced the same.

As a result of the brutal attack, the man was in terrible shape. Jesus said they left the man half-dead. This might be your situation right now—feeling half-dead in the middle of a difficult situation in life:

- Living in half of a marriage
- Trying to keep together half of a family
- Struggling to revive half of a career
- Fighting to hold on to half of your sanity

But hold on. If the thieves left the man half-dead, then it also means they left the man half-alive! There is hope. The injured man was still half-alive and might live to fight another day. And if you're feeling like you're in that half-dead situation today, I'm here to tell you the worst mistake your enemy ever made was to leave you half-dead, because there's part of you that is half-alive. And if you take the half that you *do* have and connect it with the whole of God, then you have everything you need to make it. Focus on the good, on what's left, and start from there.

Next, Jesus continued the story by describing the travelers who encounter the injured man lying there next to the road. He was too hurt to get up and walk, so he lay there in pain, alone, waiting. If someone didn't stop and help him, he was going to die. And he knew it. There's no other word for that feeling than *despair*.

Seeing injured, dying, and dead people is a normal part of the journey on Mount Everest. Hundreds of people have died in their quest to climb Everest, and many of those bodies are still there, and visible, on the mountain. And because of the danger of the climb, it's not at all unlikely that, as a climber, you'll see other climbers struggling, falling, and even dying on your way up the mountain. You may be forced to climb by other climbers who are literally in despair.

It's a terrible dilemma for a climber. Do you stop and help? There are many reasons not to. You might not be able to help if the person is ill or seriously injured (and you're not a doctor), because you don't know what sort of treatment to administer and you don't want to make things worse. Or, by trying to help, say by carrying someone down the mountain, you might possibly endanger yourself by falling or incurring a lethal injury. Or you might lose the chance to summit, wasting all the time, money, and energy you've put into the effort over the last year. In the end, the reality on Everest is that trying to help someone who's seriously injured or dying might accomplish nothing, if he or she is already too far gone, other than endangering yourself. It's a nightmarish quandary and similar to what the passersby on that road to Jericho were facing. Do I stop and help or pass by to get to my own destination safely? The truth is we all need help on life's journey. Virtually no traveler or climber gets to his or her destination without help, especially when an emergency arises (and they always do).

The first traveler to pass by, Jesus said, was a priest who "happened to be going down the same road, and when he saw the man, he passed by on the other side."[4] The reason he didn't stop was because according to the Levitical laws, as a priest he was not allowed to touch a dead body. If he did touch a dead man, he would become ceremonially unclean, and until he went through the necessary rituals to become clean again, he would not be able to carry out his job. So because the priest thought the man lying there might be dead, he avoided him and passed by on the other side. Can you imagine how the man felt?

Despair.

However, the priest had clearly misdiagnosed the situation. The man wasn't dead. He was alive and waiting for help. How often do we pass judgment on people, misdiagnosing their situations and giving up on them because they seem beyond help and hope? Perhaps you've been the one waiting for help.

Caleb Swanigan was a kid who needed help. A dysfunctional family life with a crack cocaine–addicted father led to Caleb's obsession with food. In the summer before eighth grade, he tipped the scales at 360 pounds. He was facing insurmountable odds, and he desperately needed someone to notice.

Caleb's eighth grade summer was also the summer that former Purdue football star Roosevelt Barnes, now a successful sports agent, made a decision to intervene. He stepped forward to adopt Caleb, then moved the young man to Fort Wayne, Indiana. Barnes took a chance on a kid who had no chance, and everything changed. With a new, stable, loving family, Caleb grew into what he was destined to be—a star athlete. He grew up to a monumental 6'8", slimmed down to 247 pounds, and became a star basketball player for Purdue. Roosevelt had seen something in Caleb and offered him a hand up. He took it and held on.[5] However, if Caleb had been waiting for help from this particular priest in Jesus' story, he would have been waiting a long time.

The next traveler in Jesus' story was a Levite. The Levites were descended from the tribe of Levi and historically had both priestly and political duties. He was an important person in the community, but it was the same story as the priest. The Levite looked at the man, didn't want to risk getting involved, and passed by on the other side. Maybe he was afraid the thieves were still in the vicinity, or that someone would think he'd committed the crime. He saw, but he didn't help because he didn't want the victim's issues to become his issues.

Now the dying man had been passed by two people. How often do we, who seem to be religious, pass or turn away those who need our help? Especially if they look or do things that to us are dirty, disgusting, or repulsive? When we push those who are broken and hurting away, we push them down into despair and a place of no hope.

The third traveler was a Samaritan. Since the Samaritan people were considered religiously inferior, a great chasm had developed between Jews and Samaritans, with both claiming to practice the true religion and worship the one, true God. But they didn't like or trust each other.

Ironically, though, the Samaritan was the one person who broke tradition and stopped to help the suffering man in tangible ways.

A Samaritan, as he traveled, came where the man was; and when he saw him, he took pity on him. He went to him and bandaged his wounds, pouring on oil and wine. Then he put the man on his own donkey, brought him to an inn and took care of him. The next day he took out two denarii and gave them to the innkeeper. "Look after him," he said, "and when I return, I will reimburse you for any extra expense you may have."[6]

Score one for the outsider! This Samaritan man, from a group of people looked down on and considered half-breeds, was the hero of Jesus' story. The Samaritan represents God, who always goes out of His way to get involved and help those who need it. The best picture of this is Jesus, who came down from heaven, put on human flesh, and intervened in the human story. He took on our mess. God loves us so much there are no boundaries He won't go past to reach down and pull us out of the pit. He is the definition of what we need to be safe and be saved.

Who are we really? Are we Jesus people or something totally different? Jesus people wouldn't have walked past this hurting man lying by the side of the road. And those who are hurting all around us are the norm, not the other way around.

To "take pity" on someone means to experience deep compassion, the kind of compassion that prompts you to identify with someone else no matter how different he or she is and then to intervene on that person's behalf. The Samaritan man put aside his differences so he could see, really see, the injured man who needed his help, stop to assess the situation, and then figure out how to help. It was triage, borne out of love for a fellow human being. He showed love and care for someone he'd never met before, who was different in background, culture, and religion, and who likely would not be able to ever pay him back for saving his life. It was an unselfish love with no expectations attached, like the basis for the old grant covenants. Jesus' story reveals the heart of God, whose desire is for us and who will do anything to be connected with us, heal us, and keep us safe.

Jesus finished telling the story, tying it all together for the expert in the law, with his original question about what he needed to do to inherit eternal life and be saved. "Which of these three do you think was a neighbor to the man who fell into the hands of robbers?" Jesus asked.

"The one who had mercy on him," said the expert in the law.

"Go and do likewise," said Jesus.[7]

Point made.

Being safe on Everest is all about preparing beforehand and then taking care of yourself on the mountain. It's life or death, and it's very difficult, if not life-threatening, to help another climber in distress. Many advise against it.

But the road from Jerusalem to Jericho is another kind of story altogether. This journey is also about life and death, but Jesus makes it clear we are to help others who are suffering, no matter their backgrounds, cultures, or religions. We are to take pity and have compassion. We are to offer help and hope, because that's what Jesus did for us. On the cross He took on Himself every sin, in a world system that was against God, and He took on Himself every accusation the enemy ever made against the human race. He died with us, instead of us, and He died for us—and that's how He healed us.

God is the Good Samaritan in this story. When we need Him and call out in despair, He will never pass by on the other side of the road. When we are down and suffering, because of His love for us He will always see us, take pity on us, stop and reach down, and help and heal us. May we go and do the same.

## POINTS TO REMEMBER

- A key question we all face at one point or another: How can I be saved from death and judgment? In other words, what must I do to be safe and saved?
- The truth is we all face problems and there are times we need help on life's journey.

- When difficulties arise, sometimes it can feel like you're all alone. The emotional pain of being left all by yourself in a difficult situation is worse than the pain of the actual situation.
- The Good Samaritan represents God, who always goes out of His way to get involved and help those who need it. The best picture of this is Jesus, who came down from heaven, put on human flesh, and intervened in the human story. He took on our mess.
- God loves us so much that there are no boundaries He won't cross to reach down and pull us out of the pit.
- Jesus makes it clear we are to help others who are suffering, no matter their backgrounds, cultures, or religions, with love and compassion.

## QUESTIONS TO PONDER

1. Think of a time when life knocked you down and you needed help. Who came along and gave you a helping hand?
2. Was the person who helped you someone you expected? Or someone you did not expect help from?
3. Have you ever faced a difficult situation and there was no one to help? What did it feel like to be left by yourself?
4. In the story Jesus told, how is the Good Samaritan like God?
5. What boundaries sometimes prevent us from helping others who are suffering?

# CHAPTER 13

# Reliable GPS

*I've been lost many times in my life, and I've had to
have someone guide me back on the right path.*
—JEREMY LIN

After the Second World War, Europe was a mess. While the
Allies won the war, there was suffering and chaos in almost
every country in Europe. Millions of people were separated from
their families, displaced from their towns, homes, and jobs, and
living wherever they could find shelter.

Refugee camps sprouted up everywhere. People liberated from
the death camps or fleeing the German or Russian armies were living in schools, abandoned factories, and former military barracks.
Other refugee camps were located in airport hotels, hospitals, and
even private homes.

Food for the starving crowds came from the occupying military
forces, the United Nations, the Red Cross, or other humanitarian

organizations. Many of the refugees were starving, sick, or dying. Sanitation was a problem, leading to even more illness and problems with lice. In addition, refugees were depressed, traumatized, and fearful. What would the future hold? Would they be able to find jobs or get an education? Were they safe? Would they ever be able to go back home? There was incredible uncertainty.

One survivor, a young Jewish man named Henry from a town in Poland, lost everyone in his family. He survived the initial invasion by Germany; he survived the ghetto, where every Jewish person in town was rounded up and put behind barbed wire; he survived a hellish ride on a train to a camp called Auschwitz; and, somehow he survived two and a half years in the death camp. But sixty-three members of his family did not.

When Auschwitz was liberated by Allied soldiers, Henry weighed less than ninety pounds. But he felt like God had saved his life, sent two guardian angels to watch over him, and given him a will to live. As his health returned, he took some odd jobs, including translation work for the US Army.

As Henry grew stronger, he began to think about his girlfriend, Anna. He'd met her in his hometown, and she had also survived the ghetto and the train transport. He'd caught a glimpse of her every once in a while inside Auschwitz, but he didn't know what happened to her. Did Anna survive until the camp was liberated? Did she make it through the chaos, devastation, and starvation after the war? And where was she now?

Henry had lots of questions but no way to get answers. Whole communities had been broken up, and families were scrambling to find lost members and reunite. People were moving from camp to camp looking for someone, anyone, they knew. Even though he didn't know the way, Henry knew he had to try.

Once he found a motorcycle he could afford, off he rode into the shifting sands of displaced people. Every weekend, he headed out to search for his love. The International Red Cross was putting together lists of names, trying to reunite people, and eventually the International Tracing Service collected more than one million names. Henry's girlfriend was truly one in a million.

About eight months into the search, Henry heard a rumor Anna might be in a refugee camp in Munich, Germany. He could hardly wait for the weekend to come. When Saturday morning finally arrived, he gassed up his bike and headed out on the road. His heart beat harder with each checkpoint he passed through.

Finally, Henry reached the Munich camp and knocked on the door of the official in charge. He gave his girlfriend's name, and the officer looked up at him, then down again. Then he gave a room number, pointing him in the right direction.

Henry walked, then began to run toward the room. He knocked on the door, several quick, loud raps. His heart was beating out of his chest. The door swung open. He stood there, not moving.

Dark hair, bright eyes. It was her.

Anna looked at Henry. Her eyes opened wide and her mouth flew open. She shrieked. "Oh my God. You're alive!"

She jumped into his arms. Her sisters came running, and they started screaming, too, and jumping up and down. Doors up and down the way began to open, and people poured out of their rooms, wondering what was happening. When they heard the news, they joined in and became a huge mass of people jumping and shouting for joy, hugging one another and smiling ear to ear.

"The dead man is alive," one of the sisters shouted. "The dead man is alive!"

Henry was alive. And so was his girlfriend. They'd made it—two survivors who beat the inestimable odds when so many others had not. And it was all because Henry never gave up hoping, or dreaming, or getting out and looking for the way back to the one he loved.

Two thousand years ago in Jerusalem, Jesus spent some time preparing His closest friends for a big bump in the road they were about to encounter. During the Last Supper, Jesus didn't tell them exactly what was going to happen, but He did spend some time in an important conversation with them because He knew it was time to leave and go back to His Father in heaven. After a quiet dinner, Jesus first took on the role of a servant and grabbed a towel, knelt down on the floor, and lovingly washed His disciples' feet. They were shocked at how He was humbling Himself to serve them.

Next, He began to talk, giving them some guidance and a preview of what was going to happen in the next few days. He wanted to fortify them with hope, when He knew they were going to experience the horror of His death.

"Do not let your hearts be troubled," he said. "You believe in God; believe also in me. My Father's house has many rooms; if that were not so, would I have told you that I am going there to prepare a place for you? And if I go and prepare a place for you, I will come back and take you to be with me that you also may be where I am. You know the way to the place where I am going."[1]

Their minds must have been reeling, trying to understand and respond to what Jesus was saying. But only one spoke up: Thomas. The practical one. The straight shooter. He wasn't satisfied with vague promises. He wanted more.

"Lord, we don't know where you are going, so how can we know the way?" asked Thomas.

"I am the way," said Jesus.[2]

People throughout the years have labeled Thomas as a skeptic. "Doubting Thomas," he's been called, both for this interaction and for his skepticism when Jesus appeared alive after the crucifixion.

But what I appreciate about Thomas is his honesty. He was keeping it real. His raw question represents the situation all of us have been in at one point or another. Regardless of age, race, station, or status in life, we often don't know the way, even if we pretend that we do.

It starts early in life. Who do I make friends with? Who should I play with, study with, or go to the movies with? What do I want to do when I grow up? Where should I go to school? What should I study? Where should I work? Do I believe in God? Will I follow Him? Who should I date, get engaged to, marry? Where should I live? Where should I go to church?

In adulthood, the serious decision-making continues. If anything, it gets even more intense. Some decisions are heavy, with life-changing consequences. Who will help me grow spiritually? Who do I turn to when I have problems? How do I handle difficult situations? What happens when I make this important medical decision, or that relationship choice?

What is going to happen next?

What is the best way forward?

The decisions and the choices never end. Life and its decision points rarely come with any sort of comprehensive, trustworthy instruction manual. There are so many decisions to make, and often no clear path to take. Everyone faces these decision points, both individually and corporately, whether it's in the context of a family, a business, an organization, or even a government.

The reason the world is in the shape it is today is because

we don't know the way. And in his blunt but truthful questions, Thomas called us all out on it. "Lord, how can we know the way?" It's the question of the ages.

I love how in response to that simple question, Jesus gave the answer that Thomas, and the world, desperately needs. "I am the way and the truth and the life," Jesus said. In essence, Jesus was saying He is the path to every destination, the remedy for every problem, and the answer to any and every question.

Jesus is the answer for the world today. Above Him there's no other. The way isn't a place or a plan; it is a person. Jesus is the way.

Jesus knew His friends needed some direction. We all do. Most of us like to know something about the road ahead. This is especially important for road trips. If you're of a certain age, you remember paper road maps. Yes, they were hard to fold, and they wore out or ripped along the creases, but every traveler had at least one because there was no GPS in your car or on your phone. Before you left your point of departure, you had to already know the way from experience, have detailed instructions from a friend, or have a map with the route highlighted. If you hadn't studied the map, you were likely to get lost, because it was not easy to look at the map on the fly.

Back then, maps didn't talk and tell you the way. You had to wrestle the map and fold it open to the correct spot, then trace your route. If the map wasn't detailed enough (because some maps were highway maps), you needed a street map. Some of us even invested in a Thomas Guide, a thick, heavy, floppy book of maps for a particular area or region, rich with detailed street maps. On these old-school maps, highlighters were your friend. And you had to use your brain.

Those old maps were treasures because the markings formed

a record of past journeys. But personally, I'm delighted to have a GPS because it's almost impossible to get lost (although it can still be done, if your GPS uses outdated information or occasionally, just plain gets it wrong). Clear directions and maps were, and are, essential if you wanted to find your way. How much more, then, does every single one of us need clear and helpful direction on our spiritual journey through life? The stakes are high, and God doesn't want any one of us to get lost. He's our divine GPS, the ultimate mapmaker and provider of direction, and the destination is eternity with Him, and through His Son Jesus, He made a way.

From the beginning of time, and from the moment things went wrong in the universe, everything has been pointing to Jesus. Much like the man looking for his lost girlfriend after the war heard whispers and rumors about her location, so has the world been hearing whispers about the coming of Jesus Christ. There are clues and hints in the older writings of the Bible that give us a foretaste of what is going to come, and how we will find the way.

First, God created the world and everything in it. His crowning achievement, the masterpiece of His creation, was the creation of humans. God created people in His image, put His breath into the first man and woman, and gave them dominion and authority over everything He created. The only disclaimer God gave the first man and woman was this, in Genesis 2:16–17: "You are free to eat from any tree in the garden; but you must not eat from the tree of the knowledge of good and evil, for when you eat from it you will certainly die."

Eating fruit from that particular tree was obviously not planned to be the way. But then the enemy arrived, in the form of a serpent. The enemy only wanted to do three things: steal, kill, and destroy. He tempted and misled the man and woman, enticing them to take the forbidden fruit. So the first man, Adam, and the first woman, Eve, made their choice. And from the moment they ate the fruit, things began to fall apart.

Adam and Eve knew something was wrong and were ashamed, trying hard to cover their nakedness with fig leaves. But even though God was surely upset, disappointed, and heartbroken, He still loved His people. He took animal skins and covered their nakedness. That meant He had to take the life of an innocent animal to give the skins to Adam and Eve. God initiated something called substitution; in order for Adam and Eve to live, someone had to die because without the shedding of blood, there could be no remission of sins.[3] That animal died so the man and woman could live. Even all the way back in Genesis, the first book of the Bible, God was pointing to the fact that there would be a sacrificial cover for our wrongdoing.

Adam and Eve had two sons named Cain and Abel. Cain was a farmer and Abel was a shepherd, and both boys wanted to find a way to please God. "In the course of time, Cain brought some of the fruits of the soil as an offering to the LORD. And Abel also brought an offering—fat portions from some of the firstborn of his flock. The LORD looked with favor on Abel and his offering, but on Cain and his offering he did not look with favor. So Cain was very angry, and his face was downcast."[4]

For eons, people have looked at this story and reasoned that the problem had something to do with the unique personalities of the two brothers. Abel must have had a good attitude, was humble, and loved God, so his sacrifice was pleasing. Cain, however, seemed to have a bad attitude. He was arrogant and prideful, so God rejected his sacrifice. It seems simple, if you explain it that way.

But God's response had nothing to do with Cain's and Abel's personalities, and everything to do with their individual offerings.

What Cain tried to do was give God the fruit of the soil. He tried to give something his hands had produced, something he had worked for. And God wouldn't accept it. He explains why in Ephesians 2:8–9. "For it is by grace you have been saved, through faith—and this is not from yourselves, it is the gift of God—not by works, so that no one can boast." The clue is that the way to please God has nothing to do with the work of your own hands and everything to do with the work of God.

What Abel gave God was the best of his flock. And the best of a flock of sheep are the lambs. Abel knew it was going to cost him, but he was willing to sacrifice a lamb, and that's why God accepted his offering.

Later, in the story of Abraham and Isaac, God provided another signpost to the right way. God called on Abraham with this: "Take your son, your only son, whom you love—Isaac—and go to the region of Moriah. Sacrifice him there as a burnt offering on a mountain I will show you." Abraham immediately started out to do what God asked. The reason he didn't show any shock or surprise is that he and his family were surrounded by ungodly tribes of people who routinely practiced human sacrifice to appease their pagan gods.

God had made the plan, picked the place, and prepared the sacrifice in advance. But unbeknownst to Abraham, the sacrifice was not going to be his son. God had something else in mind, but Abraham couldn't see it yet.

> Abraham took the wood for the burnt offering and placed it on his son Isaac, and he himself carried the fire and the knife. As the two of them went on together, Isaac spoke up and said to his father Abraham, "Father?"

"Yes, my son?" Abraham replied.

"The fire and wood are here," Isaac said, "but where is the lamb for the burnt offering?"

"God himself will provide the lamb for the burnt offering, my son."

With the story of Abraham and Isaac, God was pointing to Jesus. God showed us the lamb was a human. Because it was a human who sinned in the beginning, so it must be a human who was sacrificed. And in a strange turn of events, Mount Moriah was the exact same place where Jesus was crucified thousands of years later. (The place was called Mount Moriah in the Old Testament, and Calvary or Golgotha in the New Testament.)

But through His providence, and because Abraham was listening to God, believing God, and following the way, God provided a miraculous solution. Just when he was about to sacrifice his son,

the angel of the LORD called out to him from heaven, "Abraham! Abraham!"

"Here I am," he replied.

"Do not lay a hand on the boy," he said. "Do not do anything to him. Now I know that you fear God, because you have not withheld from me your son, your only son."

Abraham looked up and there in a thicket he saw a ram caught by its horns. He went over and took the ram and sacrificed it as a burnt offering instead of his son.

So Abraham called that place *The* LORD *Will Provide*.[5]

As He had promised, God provided the lamb for the sacrifice, and Isaac was saved.

Another signpost along the way took place in Egypt, when Moses was in the battle of his life—freeing the people of Israel from the tyrant, Pharaoh, who was holding them in slavery. A series of plagues had struck Egypt, and this last one would be the worst of all. Every firstborn son in Egypt was going to die. But God was going to protect the people of Israel, His people, with the blood of an unblemished lamb.

"Tell the whole community of Israel that on the tenth day of this month each man is to take a lamb for his family . . . The animals you choose must be year-old males without defect," instructed God. "Then they are to take some of the blood and put it on the sides and tops of the doorframes of the houses . . . On that same night I will pass through Egypt and strike down every firstborn of both people and animals, and I will bring judgment on all the gods of Egypt. I am the LORD. The blood will be a sign for you on the houses where you are, and when I see the blood, I will pass over you. No destructive plague will touch you when I strike Egypt."[6]

God told His people to get an innocent lamb, a lamb without spot or blemish. And the penalty for sin was going to fall on the lamb. Justice demanded death, but by means of a substitution, the lamb would die for them. Its blood had to be shed and then applied. If the blood was not applied, the death angel would still come into that house. But if the blood was applied, the death angel would pass over the house because the blood signified that death had already visited that house. Someone had already died.

God always has a plan for the way.

Adam and Eve's story showed Jesus is the way to be covered.
Cain and Abel's story showed Jesus is the way to acceptance.

Abraham and Isaac's story showed Jesus is the way to provision and promises fulfilled.

And Moses' story showed Jesus is the way to freedom and life.

There's one last signpost for the way, and it's in 2 Corinthians. "All these new things are from God who brought us back to himself through what Christ Jesus did . . . urging everyone to come into his favor and be reconciled to him. For God was in Christ, restoring the world to himself, no longer counting men's sins against them but blotting them out. This is the wonderful message he has given us to tell others. . . . For God took the sinless Christ and poured into him our sins. Then, in exchange, he poured God's goodness into us!"[7]

There is a way, and His name is Jesus. Isaiah showed us Jesus is the way to healing and wholeness. Because He loves us, Jesus took our pain and our suffering and was broken and pierced for our sins, crushed for our wrongdoings, and punished in order to bring us peace. By His wounds we are healed, and His death is for everyone. His sacrifice heals us from sin, sickness, poverty, and death of spirit, mind, and body.

Jesus, the unblemished Lamb of God, is the solution to our problems. His cousin, John the Baptist, said it best: "Look, the Lamb of God, who takes away the sin of the world."[8]

As important as Henry's journey was to find his girlfriend after the war, and as important as it is for a driver to know the correct route, it's much more essential to know the right way—make that the *only* way—to forgiveness and to eternity. The only way is God's way.

Thomas the doubter asked a simple question, wanting the answer we are all dying to know. *How do we find the way?* The way, who happened to be standing right in front of him in the flesh and talking directly to him, is Jesus.

## POINTS TO REMEMBER

- Life and its decision points rarely come with any sort of comprehensive, trustworthy instruction manual. There are so many decisions to make and often no clear path to take.
- Jesus told His disciples, "I am the way and the truth and the life." Jesus was saying He is the path to every destination, the remedy for every problem, and the answer to any and every question.
- There were hints of "the way" back in the first book of the Bible. Genesis tells the story of a substitutionary sacrifice of an animal for Adam and Eve's sin of disobedience to God.
- The stories of Cain and Abel, and Abraham and Isaac, also point to this idea of a substitutionary sacrifice for sin.
- When God's people were enslaved in Egypt, each family was instructed to sacrifice a lamb to save them from death.
- The ultimate lamb, and substitutionary sacrifice, is Jesus. His sacrifice heals us from sin, sickness, poverty, and death of spirit, mind, and body.
- The entire Bible points to this: Jesus is the way.

## QUESTIONS TO PONDER

1. Don't you wish life came with a specific instruction manual just for you and the decisions you need to make? What are some of the tactics you use to make a good decision?

2. When you hear the words, "Jesus is the way," what picture comes to mind? If you had to paint a painting, how would you portray this?

3. What was the sin Adam and Eve committed in the garden of Eden? Do you think you would have been able to resist the temptation to do the same?

4. What was Cain's sin? Why did God accept Abel's sacrifice? How can you be more like Abel in your relationship with God?

5. When Abraham was told to sacrifice his son, what happened to save Isaac? Have you ever experienced a last-minute, unexpected "save" in a difficult situation?

6. Why is Jesus sometimes called the Lamb of God?

7. The sacrifice Jesus made for us seems overwhelming. How does God want us to respond to this sacrifice?

# Living Loved

*To be loved, to be loved! Oh,*
*what a feeling to be loved!*
—Jackie Wilson, Diana Ross, Michael Bublé

When we open our hearts to God, the results are life transforming.

Like Søren lavished his love on Regine through gifts and letters, when God arrives at the door of our hearts, He comes bearing gifts.

# CHAPTER 14

# The Gift of Freedom, Part 1

*God is a God who has not given up on His people. If He wanted to
give up, He would have given up back in the Garden of Eden.*
—Kirk Cameron

It was Christmas Day, and a young woman named Petra was on
top of the world. A successful model, Petra was taking a break
from the constant travel of work and relaxing under the palm trees
on an exotic tropical vacation in Khao Lak, Thailand, with her
fiancé, Simon.

Petra and Simon were taking one last walk on the beach before
they left the resort to head home. But they noticed something
strange—the ocean waves were going the wrong way, receding
backward instead of rolling onto the beach. Petra didn't think
much of it, and the couple walked back to their bungalow. That's
when they heard the screaming.

Petra peeked outside and saw people running away from the

beach, and moments later, a massive tsunami hit the beach and rushed over the resort, breaking windows and knocking down walls. Before they could escape, Petra and Simon were sucked out into the wave and tossed about like two pieces of debris.

Petra got one last look at Simon that day before he was swept away with many other people. Then the second wave hit. "I couldn't get back to the surface to breathe," said Petra. She started swallowing water and thought she was dying as she looked at the debris above.

Suddenly, however, she popped back up to the surface and caught a breath, then felt herself being carried out to sea. As the wave pulled her along, she saw the top of a palm tree and tried to grab it but couldn't. Then she saw another, and this time she was close enough to grab it and hold on. Even though she was safe for the moment, it was a nightmare as people swept by her, waving and screaming. But no matter what she saw or heard, Petra knew she had to hang on to the top of the palm tree if she was to have a chance to survive.

Petra clung to the palm tree for hours, and finally the angry tsunami waters calmed down and receded. She ended up lying amid the debris, helpless and exhausted, her pelvis broken in several places. Finally, she was found and cared for, eventually recovering. Later, she found out that there were an estimated 280,000 victims of the tsunami, making it one of the worst natural disasters in modern history. Unfortunately, although Simon was a good swimmer, he didn't survive, and his body was found several weeks later.

Petra knew she'd been given a second chance at life, and that made all the difference. She started a foundation called Happy Hearts to rebuild the schools destroyed by the tsunami. At last count, more than a hundred schools had been constructed. "It feels like a heavy weight has been lifted off my shoulders. My life was slipping through my fingers before; now I'm living it fully in the here and now."[1]

I'm guessing Petra feels grateful to the tree that saved her life. It seemed to pop up out of nowhere, right when she needed it. While that was an extraordinary circumstance where a tree saved a woman's life, trees are in themselves beautiful and majestic things. Being in a forest with the sunlight filtering down is like walking inside of a living cathedral. Your eyes are drawn upward, and it's cool, shady, and smells good.

Trees do much more than stand around and look pretty though. Trees bear fruits and nuts, shade and protect other plants, sustain and make a home for animal life, give us firewood and lumber for building, and filter the air we breathe. In addition, over the last decade researchers have discovered that the soil underneath tree is not only filled with roots and mycelium, the fungal network that trees use to communicate with one another, but it also harbors a certain bacteria called *Mycrobacterium vaccae*. When you dig into the soil with your hands, walk in it barefoot, or even breathe it in, the bacteria increases the serotonin and norepinephrine in the human brain, acting like a dose of Prozac. That's right—soil acts like an antidepressant and boosts your mood.

All these benefits scientists are discovering show how trees and gardens function in what is, essentially, a broken world marred by sin. Can you imagine what the garden of Eden must have been like *before* sin entered the world? Imagine the benefits those first trees and plants must have offered.

Just because He wanted to, God created the most beautiful garden that's ever existed, full of trees, plants, and animals. Then, to complete the garden, He created a man and a woman to live inside of it. Adam and Eve not only took care of the garden, the garden took care of them. It was a mutually beneficial arrangement, with all creation living in perfect harmony.

The first two people on the earth were gardeners, created and trained by the original Gardener Himself, the great I Am. What a delight it must have been for God to see Adam and Eve enjoying the garden, eating the good things it provided, sleeping in leafy beds under the trees, and marveling at its beauty. God loved His garden and His two humans so much that He came in the evenings and walked around the garden with Adam and Eve. The Bible doesn't tell us what form He took or if they could see Him, but they could hear Him and they knew He was there, enjoying the garden.

In the center of the garden were two special trees: the Tree of Life and the Tree of the Knowledge of Good and Evil. When God created Adam, one of the first things He did was to tell him about the two trees at the center. "You may freely eat the fruit of every tree in the garden—except the tree of the knowledge of good and evil. If you eat its fruit, you are sure to die."[2] Adam listened, and he obeyed God. He didn't eat from the tree of the knowledge of good and evil, although he must have been familiar with both trees, as he was the caretaker of the garden. Just as a parent knows his or her children and a shepherd knows his or her sheep, so do gardeners know their gardens.

After some time alone living and working in the garden, Adam grew lonely, so God made a woman from one of Adam's ribs and brought her to the man. It was love at first sight. "'At last!' the man exclaimed. 'This one is bone from my bone, and flesh from my flesh! She will be called *woman*, because she was taken from *man*.'"[3] You can almost hear the delight in his voice. I imagine he must have said or thought something like this: *Here is someone like me, but also different from me, yet she is part of me. She is amazing. Thank You, God!*

Because Adam and Eve lived in a garden in complete harmony with nature, they were naked. Like the animals, they lived comfortably inside of their skins and did not have a concept for nakedness or covering up. No hiding their bodies, no sense of modesty or shame. Their pure and innocent worldview was perfectly aligned with nature. Nothing was missing; they had everything they needed, including each other. They were the only human beings who have yet lived who experienced this earth as God originally created it, and they didn't know any different. They had no past and couldn't see into the future. They lived in the present, and they lived in perfection. It was bliss.

Until it wasn't. The rest of the story is told in Genesis 3. One day Adam and Eve were in the center of the garden near the two trees God had planted there. They might have been working, cultivating the soil, or watering the trees, or maybe they were relaxing, talking, and enjoying each other's company. Suddenly, a serpent addressed Eve. The Bible doesn't say whether the serpent was in one of the trees or not, only that the serpent was the shrewdest of all the wild animals God had made.

"Did God really say you must not eat the fruit from any of the trees in the garden?" asked the serpent.

"Of course we may eat fruit from the trees in the garden," Eve said, seemingly unsurprised that a serpent was talking to her. "It's only the fruit from the tree in the middle of the garden that we are not allowed to eat. God said, 'You must not eat it or even touch it; if you do, you will die.'"

"You won't die!" the serpent assured the woman. "God knows

your eyes will be opened as soon as you eat it, and you will be like God, knowing both good and evil."

Eve listened to the serpent and was convinced because the fruit looked delicious to her and she wanted the knowledge the serpent spoke of. Adam, who was right there listening to the whole exchange, also ate some. The change was instantaneous. Their eyes "opened, and they suddenly felt shame at their nakedness. So they sewed fig leaves together to cover themselves."

That wasn't the only cover-up. Later, when evening fell and a cool breeze was blowing, Adam and Even heard God walking around the garden, so they hid from Him in the trees.

"Where are you?" called God. Now God, being God, knew exactly where Adam and Eve were, exactly what tree they were hiding under. He also knew what had happened. Evil had entered His perfect garden, and His emotions must have been powerful— perhaps anger and grief and hurt and disappointment all mixed up and tumbling about inside of His heart.

Adam answered. "I heard you walking in the garden, so I hid. I was afraid because I was naked."

"Who told you that you were naked?" God asked Adam. "Have you eaten from the tree whose fruit I commanded you not to eat?"

"It was the woman you gave me who gave me the fruit, and I ate it," said Adam.

Then God asked Eve, "What have you done?"

"The serpent deceived me," she said. "That's why I ate it."[4]

The terrible deed was done. Adam and Eve listened to the wrong voice and made a wrong decision that would change their lives forever. That fateful decision would also change the lives of every single human being who came after them, although they didn't yet know that. Sin had entered the world through Adam and Eve's actions, their eyes had been opened, their worldviews had changed, and they were ashamed and felt compelled to hide. Their hearts and minds were different, and nothing would ever be the same again. Because of their disobedience, bliss had been blotted out.

The true story of the Tree of Life and the Tree of the Knowledge of Good and Evil is more than a cute bedtime story we tell our children. It's more than a backdrop to the story of God and His people. It *is* the story. The story of Adam and Eve, the two trees in the garden of Eden, and the first sin is at the beginning of Genesis because everything else in the Bible hinges on it. In reality, the course of each of our lives is determined by the choice of whether we choose to live by the Tree of Life or the Tree of the Knowledge of Good and Evil. One of those trees provides abundant life and freedom if we cling to it, like Petra clung to the palm tree. The other tree means an altered worldview, resulting in a life lived in brokenness and bondage to sin resulting in permanent consequences. The problem with sin is not just the natural consequences that occur as a result of our choices. The *real* problem is that our bad choices separate us from a holy and perfect God who cannot tolerate sin. Sin leads to death—the death of our innocence and the death of our relationship with God.

Knowing that God made a beautiful garden for Adam and Eve to live in and enjoy, and that His warning to Adam was clear, we can already imagine the life God really wants us to live—an abundant life in close relationship with Him. A life of not barely surviving, but truly living. A life not of struggle and pain, but of laughter, hope, purpose, restoration, and most of all, freedom. This is the kind of life God wants you to have, and understanding the choice between the two trees means understanding the kind of life

God wants for you and how to experience that life every single day for the rest of your life.

There are many people who believe in God and who accept the free gift of salvation from Him. They yearn for forgiveness, release from their sins, and the promise of eternal life in heaven with a God who loves them. But sometimes, once a person makes a decision to believe in the name of Jesus and be saved, his or her life in Christ seems to end right there. He or she makes it through the front door but lives a miserable life because that person is not free. One of the main things Jesus came to do is to give us freedom. "It is for freedom that Christ has set us free," wrote Paul in Galatians 5:1. "Stand firm, then, and do not let yourselves be burdened again by a yoke of slavery."

Living the abundant life means living in freedom from brokenness and bondage on a day-to-day basis. I experienced this kind of freedom from a burden I carried through my childhood and younger years because of my skin color. When I was forming in the womb of my mother, the Creator saw fit to give me an extra helping of dark-chocolate color in my skin. At first I didn't know any different; my skin was my skin, and I didn't think about the color.

But as I got older, I began to be teased for my dark skin, and I noticed that my lighter-colored brothers and sisters were thought by many to be more attractive. This had a huge impact on my self-image. Other kids made fun of me, and I grew up feeling ridiculed, awkward, and unattractive, and there was nothing I could do about it. Over time, it became a terrible burden, and I battled feelings of worthlessness. I felt like I was living with shackles on with no way out.

I grew up in church and I believed in God, but I didn't really know who He was or how much He loved me. My church was traditional, with lots of fire-and-brimstone talk, and I was scared into salvation by the frequent talk about hell, the devil, and his demons. God was a stern rule maker, and I didn't feel I could measure up to His standards. Every time I messed up and did something wrong, the burden of insecurity and shame grew heavier and the shackles became tighter. I didn't know if I could ever escape. Freedom was just a concept, but not my reality.

There are so many people living in this kind of bondage. Not everyone struggles with skin color or physical attractiveness, but there are many other kinds of burdens people stagger underneath. Perhaps you've been abused or have suffered through broken relationships. Perhaps you've fought your way through substance abuse or are still right in the middle of the fight. Perhaps you've disappointed your parents or other people who've loved you. Or maybe you feel like you've failed or don't measure up in a million other ways.

But before we go any further, know this. God wants you to live in freedom, not bondage. And the difference between living a life of freedom and living a life of bondage revolves around understanding these two trees. Because a tree can save your life—just ask Petra.

## POINTS TO REMEMBER

- The first two people God created were asked to take care of God's garden, called Eden. Adam and Eve were the only human beings who have yet lived who experienced this earth as God originally created it, and they didn't know any different. They lived in perfection.

- In the center of the garden were two special trees: the Tree of Life, and the Tree of the Knowledge of Good and Evil. God told Adam not to eat from the Tree of the Knowledge of Good and Evil.
- The serpent tempted Eve and Adam to eat from the Tree of the Knowledge of Good and Evil. They gave in and disobeyed God.
- Sin entered the world through Adam and Eve's actions. Their eyes were opened, their worldviews had changed, and they were ashamed and felt compelled to hide.
- Our bad choices separate us from a holy and perfect God who cannot tolerate sin. Sin leads to death—the death of our innocence and the death of our relationship with God.
- Living the abundant life means living in freedom from brokenness and bondage on a day-to-day basis.
- The difference between living a life of freedom and living a life of bondage revolves around understanding these two trees.

## QUESTIONS TO PONDER

1. Do you like to garden? How does it feel to be outside, surrounded by God's creation?
2. Have you ever imagined what it was like to live in Eden in a world without illness, pain, sin, shame, or death? What would be different in your own life if you lived in that kind of perfect world?
3. Now imagine what it would be like to lose that perfection in one single moment. What must it have been like for Adam and Eve to be forced to leave paradise, the only home they had ever known?

4. Why did God force Adam and Even to leave the garden? Why couldn't they stay safe inside?

5. Have you ever made a terrible mistake that cost you something precious? What did that feel like? Did you wish you could take it back and have a do-over?

6. What happened when sin entered the world? What are some of the challenges we all now face because of this life-changing moment in the garden of Eden?

# CHAPTER 15

# The Gift of Freedom, Part 2

*You, my brothers and sisters, were called to be free.*
—GALATIANS 5:13

It doesn't take much to get human beings to break the rules. It can even be something as tiny as a marshmallow. In the early sixties at Bing Nursery School in Palo Alta, California, a researcher named Walter Mischel created something he called the "Marshmallow Test" to study delayed gratification, or what we often call willpower.

More than six hundred children were given the same brief instructions: "Here is a marshmallow. If you can sit here and not eat the marshmallow, in fifteen minutes I'll come back in the room and you'll get *two* marshmallows."

The researchers did the test over and over. Sometimes they used tiny marshmallows, and sometimes they used a pretzel, mint, or a cookie.

About one-third of the kids could show self-control and wait for the second marshmallow. To control their impulses, kids would cover their eyes, turn around and not look at the marshmallow, or fidget. The older the child, the more likely he or she was to be able to resist eating the single marshmallow so he or she could get two later.

But the other two-thirds of the kids couldn't wait. Some really wanted the second marshmallow and held out for a few minutes, but ultimately gave in and gobbled it down. Some kids ate the marshmallow as soon as the grown-up left the room. And a few even ate the marshmallow while the adult was still explaining the marshmallow test to them! It's not easy to turn down something delicious sitting right there in front of you, especially when no one else is watching (or at least you *think* no one is watching).

Years later, the researchers followed up on some of the kids in the original study and found something interesting. The kids who had been able to show self-control and wait the fifteen minutes for the promised second marshmallow had turned out to be higher-achieving adults with lower levels of addiction.[1] Kids who exhibited self-control between the ages of four and six turned out to be adults who practiced self-control and delayed gratification.

Another discovery was that self-control seems to be a decision of will. A child (or adult) knows what he or she is expected to do, and knows how to do it, but the child may well choose not to, for his or her own reasons. Self-control is like a muscle, and a person can choose to flex it or not. Two examples of a level of self-control that seems to vary are former President Bill Clinton and PGA golf legend Tiger Woods. Both men had tremendous self-control in certain situations (leading to incredible success), but not others (leading to incredible, and embarrassing, failures).

Both Clinton and Woods seemed to be able to choose to exert self-control when they wanted to and turn it off when they wanted to, for their own reasons. Willpower, self-control, and delayed gratification are a choice. We might have behavior patterns or habits that have been taught to us or modeled for us, or even personally developed by us, but we have the ultimate choice on an individual basis as to whether we are going to indulge in the marshmallow or wait.

But it's not easy. There are plenty of variables in the mix. What if you're hungry? What if the marshmallow looks good and smells good? What if marshmallows are your favorite snack on the planet? What if you're not sure if the second marshmallow will materialize and you believe the old saying, a bird in the hand is worth two in the bush? What if you think you might taste the marshmallow for a second (when the adult is gone) and then put it back? What if you don't trust the adult to bring the second marshmallow? What if adults have lied to you before and you trust your own self more than you trust them? And that's just the beginning, because the human mind is capable of all sorts of creative ways to break and bend the rules and indulge the flesh. Even as children.

The apostle John talked about how all this works in the book of 1 John, where he listed the three things that trip us up: the lust of the flesh, the lust of the eyes, and the pride of life. Those are the three tools of temptation that short-circuit our self-control. All sin, tricks, traps, lies, and temptations flow from these three places. Think about Adam and Eve when they decided to take and eat the fruit from the Tree of the Knowledge of Good and Evil. Genesis 3 says the woman saw the fruit of the tree was good for food (lust of the flesh), was pleasing to the eye (lust of the eyes), and also desirable for gaining wisdom (the pride of life). She was overwhelmed with the imagined taste of the fruit, the delicious beauty of the fruit, and she couldn't wait for God to give her wisdom; she wanted it right then and there, so she made a choice. She took some and ate it, along with Adam, who was there with her.

You have the same choice. The difference between living in freedom and living in bondage revolves around a choice, and you get to make that same choice. How will you choose? Which garden of Eden tree are you going to live from? The Tree of Life or the Tree of the Knowledge of Good and Evil?

When they were tempted, Adam and Eve chose to eat the fruit of the Tree of the Knowledge of Good and Evil, even though God had told them not to. God was basically saying to them, "If you change your way of thinking, if you change the way you see things, it will create separation between us. If you change your worldview, you won't be able to understand me and relate to me." The stakes were unbelievably high.

There are four truths to understand about the Tree of the Knowledge of Good and Evil. First, the fruit was more than a beautiful species of apple, orange, or pomegranate; the fruit was knowledge. The fruit that seemed so beautiful and tasty represented information, data, ideas, worldviews, and thought patterns. The fruit was the knowledge of good and evil, and knowledge impacts the way you perceive things. To have knowledge of something changes the way you see it. The fruit imparted an alternate view of the universe to Adam and Eve, and it was an instant changeover.

Second, the fruit was deadly. God didn't warn Adam and Eve that the fruit was not a good choice, or that it didn't taste good, or even that it was bad. He said it was deadly. Eating from the Tree of Knowledge, and consuming this knowledge in the pursuit of wisdom, is deadly. Eve assumed, because the fruit looked good, that it was good for food. She thought eating it would satisfy a longing for wisdom. The problem is not the desire for wisdom; it's where you get the wisdom. Adam and Eve had direct access to God and His wisdom, but they decided to try to get wisdom from another source. And that source, worldly wisdom, is deadly and separates us from God. Wisdom from the world has led to:

- Wars
- Genocides
- Slavery
- Inequality and oppression
- Greed and selfish pursuits
- Worship of other gods
- Separation from God

In contrast, God-given wisdom is life giving, protects the innocent and vulnerable, keeps a lid on selfishness and greed, and brings us closer to the God who created us and loves us.

Third, the fruit was consumed. Eve and Adam didn't just taste the fruit, they ingested it and the worldly knowledge it stood for. In the same way, we ingest worldly ideas and then sin is conceived. James, the brother of Jesus, wrote that "temptation comes from our own desires, which entice us and drag us away. These desires give birth to sinful actions. And when sin is allowed to grow, it gives birth to death."[2] It's the old "garbage in, means garbage out" idea. Whatever you put into your mind, heart, body, and soul will come out. If you ingest worldly things, then expect bad results.

One afternoon I was in the kitchen at home when our daughter, Eden, came home from a play date singing a Justin Bieber song where he's breathlessly crooning to his "baby."

I heard the words she was singing and I had a fit. "Where'd you hear that?" I asked.

I didn't want any adult male entertainer singing those sexy, breathy words to *my* baby, who was just six years old at the time. She wasn't his baby and she never will be! A long time ago, my wife and I decided we don't want our children listening to certain kinds of music or watching certain kinds of shows on TV because it will impact their lives. If worldly ideas are planted in the hearts and minds of our children, it will surely impart the kind of wisdom that will lead them away from the wisdom only God can give.

Fourth, the fruit of the Tree of the Knowledge of Good and Evil causes separation. After they'd eaten the fruit and become ashamed of their nakedness, Adam and Eve heard God walking in the garden and they hid. God didn't hide from Adam and Eve; they hid from God. God wasn't waiting behind a tree, looking for them to fail so He could judge them; "I *knew* what you were going to do." It was the other way around. They judged God! When you really know the heart of God, and you are close to Him in an intimate and loving relationship, you will run to Him, not hide from Him. The Tree of the Knowledge of Good and Evil produces shame and victimization.

Notice the shame—Adam and Eve were naked before and felt no shame. There is a difference between guilt and shame. Guilt is about what we have done—an action or actions that have broken a rule or a law. Shame is about who we are—a feeling of despair at who or what we have become. It's much more devastating and destructive. Shame makes us want to hide and causes us to do all sorts of things that keep us from connecting or reconnecting with God.

And because we're ashamed and feel worthless, we cover up,

just like Adam and Eve did with the fig leaves. As our shame grows, we need bigger and more elaborate fig leaves. Some of us borrow or purchase designer fig leaves, but they are still fig leaves. And even if we cover up, the shame is still there. The results of shame are terrible:

- Covering up and becoming focused on doing good works
- Lying, deception, and false pride
- Getting our self-worth from achievements or accomplishments
- Concentrating on our sin instead of concentrating on our Savior

Right after shame comes the victimization, when we blame others by displacing responsibility, or we blame ourselves and sink into condemnation. We're broken, so we then disqualify ourselves from a close relationship with God and from serving God and others with our gifts. We become internally focused, missing the bigger picture of what God is doing around us. We blame ourselves. And in the end, we feel rejected when it's *we* who have walked away from God. He's still there, wanting us, desiring a relationship and loving us no matter where we are at.

When shame and victimization control our lives, we feel like we can never do or be enough to please God, and neither can anyone else. It's a terrible burden to carry, and it leads to utter hopelessness for yourself and toward others around you. You can tell which tree you are living from by how you respond to other people's sin and by how you respond to your own. Eating the fruit of the Tree of the Knowledge of Good and Evil is a trap, and it leads to bondage.

But when you live from the Tree of Life, the story is different. You exchange the promise of worldly wisdom and knowledge for a relationship with God. Instead of condemning yourself and feeling like you must always do more, the Tree of Life says that Jesus has already done the work needed to bridge the gap between you and God.

Instead of continually trying to earn God's approval, you can accept that He already loves you. You're already good enough. God's love is not a conditional experience; God loves each one of us when we're still neck deep in sin. "God demonstrates his own love for us in this: While we were still sinners, Christ died for us."[3]

Tree of Life living means you don't obey out of duty or fear; you obey out of delight. Prayer, quiet time with God, and serving in a local church is no longer drudgery, or activities done to earn points with the Divine, but we do them out of love. I don't serve my wife and family because I have to but because I love to.

When we fall in love with the Lord, we follow and obey Him out of passionate love. Jesus said, "If you love me, keep my commands."[4] Think about that statement for a moment. It's divided by a comma. Which side of the comma do you live on? The side of love? Or the side of duty?

Jesus has been called the second Adam, because He was sent by God to make right what happened back in the garden of Eden. Jesus' time on earth was carefully planned in order to make a way to get us back to the Tree of Life, because the point where everything started to go wrong was the moment when Adam and Eve decided to eat from the wrong tree.

Jesus made His choice about the Tree of Life in a different garden outside of Jerusalem called the Garden of Gethsemane. The night before He was crucified, He stayed up to pray and talk to His Father, and that's when the real showdown between the devil and Jesus happened. Jesus struggled with what was going to happen to Him the next day, and then He made a choice. He chose God's way.

In yet another garden, Jesus walked out of a rich man's tomb three days after He was murdered on a Roman cross. Mary Magdalene, a follower of Jesus, was there to anoint His body. When she saw Him alive and whole, she didn't recognize Him at first. She thought Jesus was still dead, and through her tears she mistook Him for a gardener.

Jesus asked her, "Why are you weeping? Whom are you seeking?"[5]

"Sir, if You have carried Him away, tell me where You have laid Him, and I will take Him away," Mary said.

Then Jesus said her name, and she knew that voice, His voice, just as the sheep know the shepherd's voice.

She turned, saw Him, really *saw* Him, and cried out, "Teacher!" and fell at his feet because she loved Him. Then she ran to tell the others who loved Him. Jesus' early followers chose Tree of Life living. They'd fallen in love with Jesus, and it was a relationship that fueled everything they did from that point on. The good news of Jesus Christ was and is relational and transformational, not informational. Head knowledge doesn't get you to God; it's a matter of the heart, and it changes everything.

Tree of Life living means we serve God through relationships, not rules. We still do what God is calling us to do, but we do it out of our deep and growing love relationship with a God who loves us more than we can ever love Him back. "Do not think that I have come to abolish the Law or the Prophets," said Jesus. "I have not come to abolish them but to fulfill them."[6] Everything in the Bible, including the covenants, points to Jesus as the answer for our problems. The events in the garden of Eden set in motion a plan for God to make a way for us to come back into the garden we were expelled from and to taste the fruit of the Tree of Life.

Everything went wrong in that first garden, and Jesus came to make everything right again. What Adam and Eve messed up, Jesus makes right. And did you know a Tree of Life still exists? Someday, we'll get to see it. In Revelation 22, the apostle John told us what he saw in his vision of the new Jerusalem. There is a throne where God sits, and from the throne rushes a crystal-clear river. On each side of the river is a Tree of Life. The trees are covered in fruit, and guess who will get to eat the fruit from the Tree of Life?

If you love Jesus and put your trust in Him, according to Revelation 2:7, *you* will eat that fruit.

Whatever has happened in your past, it's time to move forward. Don't let your past hold you back, because there is now no condemnation to them who are in Christ Jesus. This wonderful promise is not only for us, but for those around us too. We must point people to the Tree of Life and the promise of deliverance and freedom, rather than adding to their burdens and hopelessness. "Choose life," said God in the book of Deuteronomy. "I have set before you life and death, blessings and curses. Now choose life, so that you and your children may live and that you may love the LORD your God, listen to his voice, and hold fast to him. For the LORD is your life."[7]

Hold fast to life, like Petra who held onto that palm tree while the tsunami tried its best to rip her hands away from the tree and drag her away to destruction. Hold fast and guard your heart from going back to that other tree. After you get free, you have to stay free. The enemy will try to tempt you and get you to live from the other tree, just like he did with Adam and Eve. Grab on to the Tree of Life, cling to it, and live a life of freedom.

## POINTS TO REMEMBER

- Temptation comes in different forms. The apostle John talked about the tools of temptation in the book of 1 John: the lust of the flesh, the lust of the eyes, and the pride of life.
- There are four truths around the Tree of the Knowledge of Good and Evil: the fruit was knowledge, the fruit was deadly, the fruit was consumed, the fruit caused separation.
- When you really know the heart of God, and you are close to Him in an intimate and loving relationship, you will run to Him, not hide from Him. The Tree of the Knowledge of Good and Evil produces shame and victimization.
- Shame leads to a cover-up, lying, feelings of inadequacy, a pattern of sin, and victimization. When shame and victimization control our lives, we feel like we can never do or be enough to please God, and neither can anyone else.
- When you live from the Tree of Life, you exchange the promise of worldly wisdom and knowledge for a relationship with God.
- Tree of Life living means we obey out of love and we serve God through a relationship, not rules.
- If you love Jesus and put your trust in Him, according to Revelation 2:7, you will eat the fruit of the Tree of Life.

## QUESTIONS TO PONDER

1. The tools of temptation involve both uncontrollable desire for what you cannot have and an appetite for power. Think about areas in your life that are vulnerable to one or the other of these.

2. The fruit from the Tree of the Knowledge of Good and Evil was more than just fruit. Eating it set in motion changes that shook the universe. Can you summarize the changes?

3. After Adam and Eve sinned, what did they do next?

4. What are some of the results from hiding out after you've done something you know God isn't pleased with? Does hiding work?

5. What does it mean to live from the Tree of Life?

6. What do you think the fruit of the Tree of Life will be like? Create a picture in your mind of what it might look like, smell like, and taste like. Isn't it amazing to know that we get to enjoy it?

# CHAPTER 16

# The Gift of Hope

*Hold fast to dreams,*
*For if dreams die*
*Life is a broken-winged bird*
*That cannot fly.*
—LANGSTON HUGHES

The story of Jean-Robert Cadet is the story of an outsider. When he was four years old, his mother died and he was given to another family. He wasn't adopted or fostered though. Jean-Robert was a *restavek*, meaning a household slave. When he was forced into child slavery, he lost everything, including any connections to his former life.

In Haiti, children at risk are often absorbed into a difficult life as a servant, with no rights, family identity, or access to education. *Restavek* comes from the French expression *rester avec*, or "to stay with," and the system is a holdover from the island's French colonial culture. Restavek children usually sleep on the floor, eat leftover scraps (when there are some), haul water, do heavy cleaning, and are often treated harshly without much hope for a future.

Jean-Robert served the family he was given to until he was fifteen years old. He was "lent out" to work for friends and neighbors, abused, and denied love and affection. Jean-Robert doesn't know his true age, and he described feeling like "the lowest of the low, just treated like dogs."[1]

Finally, when he was fifteen years old, he escaped. The family he served immigrated to the United States, leaving Jean-Robert behind. Somehow he found a way to follow them and then moved back in with them, still in his role as a restavek. He didn't know what else to do.

But something happened to change everything—the family discovered Jean-Robert was legally required to enroll in school while he was in the United States. When he finally started school, Jean-Robert's eyes were opened to his plight and to the possibilities awaiting him through education. He began to dream of a different life.

The family soon kicked him out, and he became homeless, but later he graduated from high school, joined the army, and went to college. Since then, Jean-Robert has earned a Master's degree in French literature, written a book about his experiences,[2] addressed the International Labor Organization at the United Nations, testified before US Congress, and appeared on the *Oprah Winfrey Show*, CNN, and *60 Minutes*. His goal? "To eradicate child slavery in Haiti."[3]

Not only did Jean-Robert escape slavery and begin to hope for a different sort of future, but he wants to help other children in the same situation have hope for their futures too. It's a lifelong journey to change a culture that permits slavery, but Jean-Robert wants others to have the same opportunities he found: to grow up, be free, get an education, and live a meaningful life. It can be a long and difficult journey, but it's worth it to be restored to a life of freedom and purpose.

Jean-Robert's story might resonate with you if you've ever felt trapped in an existence with little meaning or purpose and seemingly no way out. It's a difficult way to live when you are stuck and feeling hopeless. But there is hope, and for Jean-Robert hope came in the form of the opportunity for education. Going to school opened his eyes, and that's what God does for us. Our eyes have to be opened to the hope in front of us. Too many people go through life shrouded in hopelessness and despair instead of hope.

Not everyone is open to living with hope. My wife and I once had dinner with a family whose children went to the same school as our kids. The conversation turned toward a certain television preacher known for preaching and teaching a hope-filled, optimistic message. They said they didn't "get it." They came from a church with a strong tradition of preaching judgment, fire, and brimstone, and their faith was grounded in judgment.

But I didn't quite get *them* or their outlook, because the cross itself is a message of hope. Jesus offers hope, and if we want to embrace who Jesus really is, we live with hope, and no one can take that from us.

So many people are consumed with their problems, living in a mix of anger, despair, bitterness, and hopelessness. But there is a better way to live.

A small but powerful book in the Bible tells a three-thousand-year-old story of an ordinary woman named Ruth who was in a bad situation—like Jean-Robert she had lost everything, felt stuck, and couldn't see a way out to a different kind of life. Ruth needed restoration. She needed a powerful dose of possibility, of *what if?* and *why not?* She needed hope.

Ruth was a young woman who lived in a country called Moab on the other side of the Dead Sea from Judah, where the people of Israel lived. During a famine, a man, his wife, and their two sons moved from Bethlehem, a town in Judah, to Moab. Sometime after the move the man died and left his wife, Naomi, with two sons. The two boys grew up and married two Moabite girls named Orpah and Ruth. But after ten years of marriage the boys died too, leaving Naomi, Orpah, and Ruth to fend for themselves.

In that day, life was difficult for women on their own, and widows often had to rely on handouts from others. To further complicate her situation, since Naomi lived in a foreign land she was separated from her extended family who would make sure she was taken care of. So when Naomi heard conditions in Bethlehem had improved, she decided to return home after her long absence.

But then a surprise—her two daughters-in-law asked to go to Bethlehem with her. Naomi knew they were young enough to remarry and perhaps have children with their new husbands, so she blessed them, prayed that God would give them new families, and told them to stay in Moab.

But Orpah and Ruth loved their mother-in-law and felt connected to her. They didn't want to leave her. Naomi had introduced them to a different kind of God who loved and cared for His people, unlike the god the Moabites worshipped, named Chemosh. The worship of Chemosh was often associated with child sacrifice, so learning about Naomi's God must have been a ray of hope for the two Moabite women who were more familiar with an angry, frightening, demanding God.

So when faced with the choice to leave Moab and follow Naomi back to Bethlehem in Judah, the decision was easy. "No, we want to go with you to your people," the two young women said at first.

In the end Orpah was unwilling to leave her native country, so she kissed her mother-in-law goodbye and went back home to her family. That's the last we hear of her.

But the other daughter-in-law, Ruth, would not be deterred. She clung tightly to Naomi, knowing there must be something better ahead.

"Look," Naomi said to her, trying to dissuade her, "your sister-in-law has gone back to her people and to her gods. You should do the same."

"Don't ask me to leave you and turn back," Ruth said with determination. Then she made a solemn pledge that almost sounds like a covenant. "Wherever you go, I will go; wherever you live, I will live. Your people will be my people, and your God will be my God."

At that, Naomi gave in. When she saw Ruth was determined to go with her, she said nothing more to try to talk her out of it.[4] So the two women set out on a journey back to Bethlehem and back to the land of the God of Israel.

This true story of these three women is the story of three different ways people often respond to feeling stuck and hopeless in a situation. The first is the young widow Orpah, whose name means "turning the back." Orpah is the picture of a person who is not ready and willing to leave a familiar place or situation, no matter how difficult or hopeless it is. Orpah loved her kinfolk more than she loved the God she'd been introduced to through her mother-in-law, Naomi, and so she turned her back on a future with God.

Next is Naomi, the mother-in-law. Naomi's name means "pleasant," but after losing her husband and two sons to untimely deaths, she began to call herself Mara, which means "bitter." She had lost everything, felt like she was left with nothing, and was hurt and angry. Calling herself "bitter" probably means she was angry at God and blamed Him for what had happened when she moved to Moab. She yearned for restoration, but she was stuck.

The third woman was the other young Moabite widow, Ruth. Her name means "friend of God." Ruth somehow had hope when the other two women didn't. She sensed that there was a future for her, and that future was in the land of the God she had learned about from her mother-in-law. So when everything was taken away from her, Ruth decided to leave her family, friends, and community and follow her mother-in-law to a foreign country that might not be welcoming.

Ruth was open to the possibilities of what God had in store for her. When times were tough, Ruth put on her boots, hitched up her skirts, and leaned in. God was her friend, and in Him she had hope. She obeyed and followed God's call, and she made two key decisions:

1. Not to allow anything or anyone to deter or distract her from the high calling of God. While Orpah couldn't leave her family or her old gods, Ruth made the decision to leave.
2. Not to allow the trials and testings of life to bring bitterness and resentment against God, as Naomi had.

Ruth's story is a story of immigration. Not only was she leaving the only country she'd ever known, but she was heading into an uncertain situation. First, Moabites were not typically allowed to enter or participate in a Jewish community. She was heading into a potentially hostile situation. Also, Naomi and Ruth were arriving with nothing. They were impoverished widows.

Finally, they were exhausted from the journey, hungry and still grieving the loss of their husbands and of Orpah. Their decision to leave Moab had cost them an important relationship, taking their little family of widows from three members down to just two. Naomi and Ruth would be arriving in Bethlehem and immediately be dependent on others for food, shelter, and kindness.

Ruth's story is also a story of hunger. Not only was she physically hungry when she journeyed to Bethlehem, but she was hungry at the soul-level. Jesus once reserved a special blessing for the hungry in a sermon: "Blessed are those who hunger and thirst for righteousness, for they will be filled."[5] Ruth had lost everything, she had been humbled, and she had realized how much she needed God. Her hunger for God propelled her out of a stuck place of tragedy and loss and into a whole different life where there was a small ray of hope. And his name was Boaz.

Boaz was a wealthy, successful farmer in Bethlehem whose name means "a mighty man." *Mighty* means powerful, strong, brave, valiant, and heroic. Boaz also happened to be a kinsman of Naomi, meaning they were distant relatives but part of the same extended family through Naomi's husband who had passed away.

As fate would have it, Ruth and Naomi had arrived at the height of the barley harvest, and Ruth asked her mother-in-law if she could go out into the fields and pick up the stalks of grain left behind by the harvesters. Naomi gave her consent, and Ruth "found herself working in a field that belonged to Boaz."[6] While she was there, Boaz arrived to check on the harvesters and noticed Ruth working hard.

"Listen, my daughter," he said. "Stay right here with us when you gather grain; don't go to any other fields. Stay right behind the young women working in my field. See which part of the field they are harvesting, and then follow them. I have warned the young men not to treat you roughly. And when you are thirsty, help yourself to the water they have drawn from the well."

"What have I done to deserve such kindness?" asked Ruth, falling at his feet and thanking him. "I am only a foreigner."

"Yes, I know," said Boaz. "But I also know about everything you have done for your mother-in-law since the death of your husband. I have heard how you left your father and mother and your own land to live here among complete strangers. May the LORD, the God of Israel, under whose wings you have come to take refuge, reward you fully for what you have done."[7]

*Wait, what?!* Here was a foreign woman, a widow, penniless, picking scraps of barley out of the field to go home and make into cakes for herself and her mother-in-law, and all of a sudden she was noticed? Ruth was not only noticed here, but she was commended, she was protected, she was rewarded, and she was blessed. Boaz, a mighty man of God, welcomed her into her new community because not only did he recognize her difficult situation, but he recognized her love for God and he blessed her for it. The anonymous immigrant widow was suddenly noticed and elevated because of her faith.

Ruth truly was a friend of God, and Boaz realized it and called it out for all to hear. Ruth was hungry for God and submissive to her mother-in-law, Naomi, and because of her friendship with God, she had matured into someone whose hope was in the Lord and His plan for her life. Thanks to God's perfect, providential timing, that plan was about to become a reality through Boaz.

Just as God directed Jean-Robert Cadet from Haiti to an education and a new life in the United States, God led and directed Ruth from Moab to this one particular barley field in Bethlehem during a barley harvest. In the process God had directed her to Boaz, this kinsman of Naomi. And Boaz, who also loved the Lord, fell in love with Ruth. It was all part of God's plan.

There were no coincidences here. "The earth is the LORD's, and everything in it," wrote David in Psalm 24:1. This barley field was ultimately owned by God, and He put Ruth and Boaz together. Because both Ruth and Boaz were friends with God, hungry for God, submissive to God, and desired by God, they were right in the center of God's plan, and He led them to each other. Ruth's hope was in the Lord and she went from a tragic and terrible situation where she had nothing, to meeting a mighty man of God who had fallen in love with her and who would now give her everything.

Poor Orpah—she missed out! And Naomi almost did when she tried to send Ruth back home. But Ruth wasn't about to miss out on what God had in store for her. She leaned in and grabbed onto the tail end of God's plan, like the woman who needed healing who grasped onto Jesus' robe and wouldn't let go. Ruth was an outsider, but her determination to grab onto God and His plan made her an insider.

Fast-forward and shortly thereafter, Ruth and Boaz fell in love and got married. Being an honorable man, he followed the laws of the land and purchased all property that had belonged to Naomi's husband and two sons. Under this system, if Ruth had a son with Boaz, then her son would carry on the family name and inherit any family property.

When the news was shared at the town gate, the people of the community recognized what was happening and rejoiced, embracing Ruth with joy and open arms. "We are witnesses," the people shouted. "May the LORD give you descendants by this young woman."

The people ended up getting their wish. Boaz and Ruth had a baby boy. He was a gift from God to redeem Ruth's losses and to bless her for her faith and hope in God. The baby was loved by his grandmother, Naomi, who cared for him as if he were her own. The women of the town recognized God at work in Ruth's and Naomi's lives and said, "Praise the LORD, who has now provided a redeemer for your family! May this child be famous in Israel. May he restore your youth and care for you in your old age. For he is the son of your daughter-in-law who loves you and has been better to you than seven sons!"[8]

Not only had Ruth's life been restored and changed by her hope in God's plan, but so had Naomi's life. And it went even further than that. The results of Ruth's hope and trust in God went national, and then international, because that little baby boy who came from the unlikely love relationship of Ruth and Boaz grew up to be a man named Obed. And Obed was the father of Jesse, who was the father of King David.

When Ruth pledged herself to Naomi and to Naomi's God, she had no idea that someday her little baby boy would grow up to be the grandfather of King David, a man after God's own heart who ruled over Israel. Further, King David was the ancestor of the Messiah, Jesus Christ. That means an ordinary woman named Ruth, who was a Moabite by birth and a foreigner among the people of Israel, plus a widow, became an ancestor of the Lord Jesus Christ. And Jesus, the Son of God, came to set all of us free from sin and death.

Ruth became one of four women named in the bloodline of

Jesus, and all were outsiders with problematic pasts. All because Ruth decided to stick with Naomi and her God, choosing the way of hope.

Now *that's* what hope can do for you when you embrace it. God wants you to know there's something better ahead no matter your past, because Jesus changed the game from a struggle of trying to relate to God through legalism and the law. Instead, the path of hope goes through Jesus, and now we operate *from* His love, rather than *for* it. Hope is a gift God comes bearing to those who love Him.

## POINTS TO REMEMBER

- So many people are consumed with their problems, living in a mix of anger, despair, bitterness, and hopelessness. But there is a better way to live!
- This true story of the three women in the book of Ruth is the story of three different ways people often respond to feeling stuck and hopeless in a situation. You can give up, you can continue on but with bitterness, or you can push forward in hope.
- Ruth's story is also a story of hunger. Not only was she physically hungry when she journeyed to Bethlehem, she was also hungry at the soul-level.
- Ruth's hope was in the Lord, and she went from a tragic and terrible situation where she had nothing to meeting a mighty man of God who fell in love with her and who would now give her everything.
- The results of Ruth's hope and trust in God meant she became an ancestor of King David and of Jesus.

- Ruth became one of four women named in the bloodline of Jesus. All were outsiders with problematic pasts. All because Ruth decided to stick with Naomi and her God, choosing the way of hope.
- No matter your past, Jesus changed the game from the struggle of trying to relate to God through legalism and the law, to relying on hope, all because of His love.

## QUESTIONS TO PONDER

1. In a hard situation, how do you typically react? Are you calm and cool or more emotional and reactive? (There's no right answer here. We all react differently in difficulties.)
2. When you read about the three women in Ruth and the way each reacted to her life situation, which one resonated with you most? Can you picture yourself reacting more like Orpah, Naomi, or Ruth?
3. Have you ever felt hungry for more of God? How did this hunger come out? What did you do to fill it?
4. Ruth's story is a story with a surprise ending. Who could imagine such a fairy-tale ending for this poor immigrant widow? Do you feel sorry for Orpah, the daughter-in-law who missed out on the blessing? What could Orpah have done differently?
5. Women were not often named in genealogies of the ancient world. Why do you think God chose to name Ruth in the genealogy of David and Jesus Christ?
6. In Ruth, God found someone who loved and trusted Him. Does He find that in you? If you continue to grow in your love and trust of God, how might He use you in the future?

CHAPTER 17

# The Gift of Favor

*Favor: an act of kindness beyond what is due or usual, blessings,*
*special benefits, demonstrated delight, a token of love.*
(FROM THE LATIN *FAVERE*, "TO SHOW KINDNESS TO")

It was another long night for Cayla, a server at a busy restaurant in Waikiki. She had moved to Hawaii from Santa Rosa, California, to go to college. But the high cost of living in the islands, plus her student loan payments, forced her to abandon school and work two waitressing jobs just to pay the bills.

One evening, Cayla was serving a party of three from Australia, made up of two friends and a ten-year-old girl. As she served the small group, Cayla was her usual friendly self, so when the two friends asked why she had moved to Hawaii, she told them about her dream to go back to school.

Cayla enjoyed the chat and the friendliness of her customers, but she never expected anything more. That's why she was shocked when she collected the two-hundred-dollar tab and saw the tip: *four hundred dollars*. The extravagant tip was double the amount of the dinner bill.

In complete shock, Cayla decided she wanted to say thank you. She remembered where her customers were staying from the dinner table conversation, so she wrote a thank-you letter and dropped it off for them at the front desk of the hotel. She never expected to see them again, but she knew she would always remember these complete strangers who wanted to bless her with something far beyond what she deserved for her work.

So she was really surprised when her customers showed up at the restaurant the next night with an even more incredible, extravagant gesture. They told Cayla they were going to give her ten thousand dollars in order to pay off her student loans and give her a nest egg for her future college education.

At first she refused the offer, but the Australians ultimately convinced Cayla their gesture was as much for their own sense of joy and satisfaction as it was for hers.[1]

Cayla not only accepted the unmerited gift from her benefactors, but she believes it truly changed her life and showed her that good people, and generosity, do exist in this world. An anonymous waitress struggling to survive was noticed by people who cared about her and her problems. It's an unforgettable story.

Unexpected favor like Cayla experienced is not life as usual for most people. The older we get, the more it can feel like life is a struggle and we fight our battles during the day, then rest at night, nursing our bruised hearts and souls. It can be a tough world out there when you're going it alone, independent of God's plan and guidance. But just like Cayla, you, too, can experience favor like you have never known before.

It's time to get serious about the favor of God for your life, because God's favor is the key to your turnaround and breakthrough. Those struggles and battles you've been fighting in your relationships, with your health, your finances, at work, or in your daily life are in need of God's favor. Many of you have heard this phrase, but you've never really understood its meaning. Yet the favor of God is so important. In the Old and New Testaments, the lives of critical heroes of the faith all turned in an incredible flash on the supernatural favor of God, including Moses, David, Daniel, Mary, Peter, Paul, and many more.

Favor can make the difference between:

- success and failure
- hope and despair
- joy and regret

One day of favor is worth a thousand days of labor because when the favor of God is on your life, God can do for you in one day what it would take years to accomplish on your own. The favor of God can change rules on your behalf. It can cause people to go out of their way to bless you (whether they like you or not). It can cause doors to open no matter how many times those doors have closed before. And it can create opportunities.

God's favor on your life is not based on your background, looks, or personality. It's not just for a certain type of person. God's favor is for everyone: truck drivers, school teachers, engineers, cooks, administrative assistants, sales people, nurses, stay-at-home moms and dads, retirees, bankers, lawyers, and mechanics. God's favor can fall on men and women, boys and girls, moms and dads, grandmas and grandpas, single people, married people, urban people, country people, Republicans, Democrats, Libertarians, Green Party and Tea Party folks, and independents. It's for left wing, right wing, and no wing.

Remember this: the favor of God is available for all who accept His love and enter into relationship with Him.

This is why David said in Psalm 5:12, "Surely, LORD, you bless the righteous; you surround them with your favor as with a shield." Remember the famous phrase, "Shields up!" in the Star Trek movies and televisions shows? When the enemy approach was detected, the battle shields were activated and moved into place to protect the Federation starships against enemy attacks. God's favor is your shield, and that favor is God's gift to you. But just like on Star Trek, you have to "activate" your faith in order to believe God's promise of favor and to expect that favor.

Let's start with what the word *favor* means. Favor appears in the first book of the Bible, and the Hebrew word is *sa'ah*, which means to gaze steadily with interest, and to give special attention and great benefits to. The word doesn't mean a casual or disinterested glance, as might happen when you're out and about, seeing other people, but not really *seeing* them. When God grants someone favor, He takes a keen interest in that person. He watches, studies, and fixes His gaze on that person, then gives special attention and great benefits to him or her.

The favor of God is when God fixes His gaze on you, takes a keen interest in you, and gives you special attention and benefits. Favor takes place inside a relationship, and favor is released in an atmosphere where there is trust. The more you grow close to God and learn to trust God, the more of His favor will be released in your life.

While Cayla was a young woman who was blessed with favor,

there's another young woman blessed with favor ten thousand times greater. Her name was Mary, and she is probably the most famous woman who's ever lived. She is also the one woman in biblical history who had more favor with God than anyone else.

We don't know much about Mary's early life, but we do know she had so much favor with God that she was chosen to become the mother of Jesus Christ. She had so much favor God chose her to give birth to, nurture, and raise the Savior of the world. There was never another woman like Mary, and there never will be.

Most biblical scholars agree that Mary was about sixteen years old when her story begins in Luke 1. The first mention of Mary is in verse 27 when the angel Gabriel visited her and said, "Greetings, you who are highly favored! The Lord is with you." The *Amplified Bible Classic Edition* adds another component to the end of verse 28: "The Lord is with you! Blessed (favored of God) are you before all other women [God had a choice]." Later in the conversation, Gabriel reemphasized her favor with, "Mary, you have found favor with God."

Mary could not have missed the message. God knew her, meaning He had focused on her with special attention, and He was about to bless her in an incredible way. He was able to do this because they had a relationship already and she believed in, followed, and trusted God. She loved God with all her heart, soul, and mind because she knew and accepted God's love. She knew Him well enough to trust Him and His plan for her life, and so God felt comfortable enough in the relationship and in her trust to favor her with His only Son. She had caught God's attention and His favor.

After Gabriel left, Mary went to see her cousin, Elizabeth, who reinforced the idea of God's favor. "You are blessed because you believed that the Lord would do what he said," she told Mary.[2]

Then Mary responded with a song of praise: "Oh, how my soul praises the Lord. How my spirit rejoices in God my Savior! For he took notice of his lowly servant girl, and from now on all generations will call me blessed."[3] Because of God's favor, Mary had gone from an ordinary, anonymous teenage girl to a young woman whose name would never be forgotten.

But how did Mary become so favored? What was it about her that positioned her to receive that kind of favor from God? Why did God give her that level of staggering favor? Surely there were other women in the town of Nazareth, or the region of Galilee, or in the country of Judea, who loved and worshipped God. Why this young woman?

Because God favors people who are:

- Willing to be faithful
- Willing to believe
- Willing to allow God to fill in the blanks
- Willing to be stretched

To be faithful means to be loyal or steadfast in your allegiance. A friend of mine had a grandmother named Ruby who suffered a severe stroke in her late seventies. She had loved and served God her whole life and was a loyal member of her church, a prayer warrior, and a loving friend to all. Her stroke affected her movement and speech, and at first she couldn't move or say anything at all.

But after several months in rehabilitation, Ruby began to regain some movement. Her speech was slower in returning, and for many months she could only say three words: "Thank You, Jesus." Ruby couldn't say hello, goodbye, or even yes or no. But she could quietly say, "Thank You, Jesus," and she whispered this short phrase over and over, blessing everyone within hearing. Ruby was faithful to God, and even in difficult circumstances, her lifelong faith was on display.

Mary had that same kind of faith, and more. What is evident is that Mary didn't suddenly become faithful after God reached down and chose her to be the mother of Jesus. Instead, God chose her in part because she had already proven herself to be faithful. How do we know this?

First, Mary kept herself sexually pure. She was a virgin at the time of the angel's visit. At the age of sixteen, when many girls in that era were already married or hoping to be, Mary had most likely experienced temptation already, but she chose to honor God and remain pure.

Next, notice what Mary called herself—the "Lord's servant." Having a servant's heart and attitude, and being ready to express it during the visit of an angel, means she had committed herself to God a long time before. You don't just embrace servanthood overnight. It's a life choice at the beginning of a journey with God, and Mary had made that choice sometime in the past.

Also, look at what Mary called God. Based on the words she used for God, she had a close relationship with Him and was familiar with the Scriptures and Jewish traditions. When talking about God, she called Him the Lord, God my Savior, the mighty One, and holy. She glorified Him and rejoiced in Him, reflecting a faithful, committed relationship.

As a result, God had been watching her faithfulness for some time. God knew her habits, her spirit, her history, her routines, and her demeanor. He knew the condition of her heart and that she was faithful before He placed Jesus in her belly. God knew if

Mary could be faithful before He gave her Jesus, she would remain faithful after He entrusted Jesus to her care. Her faithfulness is what attracted God's favor.

So many of us desire God's favor, but our approach is more like this: *God, I promise I will be faithful after You bless me with . . .* (then fill in the blanks with a husband/wife, a raise at work, a financial blessing to get out of debt, a positive outcome in a legal issue, etc. You get the picture).

The big question regarding the heart of God is, *if* you get favor, can you be trusted? Because God's favor is precious, valuable, and significant, God's favor starts with your faithfulness.

You must also be willing to believe in God and His favor. When Gabriel showed up to deliver the message to Mary, she believed him, positioning herself to receive God's favor. "May it be to me as you have said," she responded to Gabriel. In other words, Mary was saying, I believe you. That was the moment of breakthrough, and this is critical because when God speaks, He speaks promises. But the question that will determine favor and breakthrough is, do you believe it?

God has given you a book full of His promises. Do you believe it?

Noah believed God.
Abraham believed God.
Moses believed God.
Ruth believed God.
David believed God.
Esther believed God.
Mary believed God.
Do *you* believe God?

In addition to being faithful and believing, you must be willing to allow God to fill in the blanks. Mary believed the Word of the Lord, but at the same time she had no clear explanation for how God was going to do what He said He was going to do. She had a promise from the angel, but she didn't have the process. That's why she asked, "But how can this happen? I am a virgin."[4]

Mary knew enough about the birds and the bees and how things worked between a man and a woman to know that this was going to be something different than what she knew. But even though she had absolutely no idea how she was going to get pregnant and bear a special baby, she still responded with, "May it be done to me according to your word."[5] In other words, she was saying, "I don't understand all the details, but I trust that God will fill in the blanks."

This is so critical because when God speaks, He speaks with promise. But what He often does not talk about is the process. So you can find yourself holding on to a promise and having absolutely no idea about the process. Yet it's okay not to understand the process as long as you can trust God to fill in the blanks. "The eyes of the LORD range throughout the earth to strengthen those whose hearts are fully committed to him," explains 2 Chronicles 16:9. God was saying that He is looking for people who are faithful, who believe, and who will open themselves up to allow God to work in and through them to accomplish His purposes.

But what we often do is begin to doubt because we see the circumstances and situations around us don't line up with the promise God is giving us. When there are too many blanks and missing pieces, it's hard for us to fully commit. But favor falls on those who trust God to take what we have and supernaturally do what only He can do.

If everything is perfect, if our lives are going well and all relationships, finances, health, and jobs situations are operating smoothly, then we don't feel like we need God or His favor. Problems, difficulties, and trials give Him room to work. When favor hits your life, it changes things regardless of what's going on around you.

Favor creates opportunities, changes rules and regulations on your behalf, and restores to you everything that has been taken from you. Mary experienced this when, out of nowhere, God gave her the opportunity to be the mother of the Messiah, the rules for bearing a baby out of wedlock were suddenly altered for her, and what she lost in terms of her reputation and community standing were given back to her and multiplied many times over with the events to come.

People rewarded with God's favor are people, like Mary, who are willing to be stretched. Being stretched means getting out of your comfort zone and taking on challenging, and sometimes uncomfortable, changes in order to grow into God's plan for your life. For Mary, this started with the upcoming pregnancy itself. Her body would go through intense changes—weight gain, swollen feet, and an enlarging belly. She knew this would happen—she'd seen it all around her in the women in her community who were with child, but she was willing to do it. Others were not, and that's precisely why they were not chosen, and favored, like Mary.

Some people don't want to have children at all simply because they don't want to go through the physical or lifestyle changes required, so they're not willing to give birth. And some people don't want to pursue God's favor, because they don't want their lives to change in order to receive it, so they're not willing to give birth to anything. But if you really do desire favor, you have to be willing to be stretched.

The prophet Isaiah talked about the stretching process when he addressed the city of Jerusalem about God's favor. "Enlarge the place of your tent, stretch your tent curtains wide, do not hold back; lengthen your cords, strengthen your stakes. For you will spread out to the right and to the left."[6] He was promising God's favor and that God was going to bless His people beyond their current capacity to receive. Favor increases the more you grow and stretch and are willing to accept and receive what God is going to do.

It's important to pray for favor and to expect favor, but you never know exactly when it's going to happen. So we live in faith, trusting God to see and focus on us and to give us the favor He's promised us, but not knowing when it's going to show up or what it's going to look like. Favor does not mean life will always be easy; Mary suffered tragedy, yet God's favor followed her and He lovingly walked her through her life's difficult circumstances. Favor is both a promise from God, so we know it's going to happen, and at the same time a mystery, because we don't know where or when.

Cultivate a heart like Mary's—faithful, trusting, expectant, submissive, obedient, willing, and passionately in love with God. Because living like that unleashes the power of what can happen when God's favor rests directly on you. A nobody can become a somebody with the favor of God empowering him or her to do something unique, extraordinary, and world changing. God is in the business of giving favor; make sure you're ready to receive it.

## POINTS TO REMEMBER

- Favor means an act of kindness beyond what is due or usual, blessings, special benefits, demonstrated delight, a token of love.
- God's favor is the key to your turnaround and breakthrough. Those struggles and battles you've been fighting in your relationships, with your health, your finances, at work, or in your daily life are in need of God's favor.
- The more you grow close to God and learn to trust God, the more of His favor will be released in your life.
- Mary, the mother of Jesus, was called "highly favored."
- God watched Mary, knew her faithfulness, and that's what attracted God's favor. God favors those who are willing to be faithful, willing to believe, willing to allow God to fill in the blanks, and willing to be stretched.
- If everything was perfect, with relationships, finances, health, and job situations operating smoothly, then we wouldn't feel like we need God and we wouldn't merit His favor. Problems, difficulties, and trials give Him room to work.
- Cultivate a heart like Mary's—faithful, trusting, expectant, submissive, obedient, willing, and passionately in love with God.

## QUESTIONS TO PONDER

1. Have you ever been someone's favorite? How did that make you feel?

2. Is there an area of your life that could use God's favor right now? Think about it, then ask Him to show you how you can gain His favor in that situation today.

3. What does it take for more of God's favor to be released in your life?

4. Why was Mary called "highly favored?" How could she have merited this distinction at such a young age?

5. If our lives are perfect, we don't need God. Does that make a difference in your wishes and dreams for your own life?

6. How can you cultivate a heart more like Mary's, so you, too, can be "highly favored"?

# CHAPTER 18

# The Gift of Forgiveness

*When you forgive, you in no way change the past—*
*but you sure do change the future.*
—BERNARD MELTZER

One of the most inexplicable benefits of following God, and something that mostly defies logic, is forgiveness. God has the capacity, and the love, to wipe the slate clean of our bad decisions, foolish behavior, and hurtful and deliberate rejection of Him. It's an amazing benefit, and it makes no sense.

God forgives great humanitarians, and He forgives hardened, selfish criminals. He forgives high achievers, and He forgives nobodies. He forgives people who turn to Him as children, and people who reject Him their whole lives and then repent at the last second. God is a God of forgiveness, and He practices it all the time, day in and day out, year after year. We don't deserve His forgiveness, and it makes no sense.

When Jesus was hanging on the cross, He talked to the criminals dying on either side of him. Both were guilty of the crimes they were being executed for, and one asked for forgiveness. Jesus, the One who was truly innocent, forgave this one who was guilty, and it makes no sense.

And because we are forgiven, we are expected to forgive others. One of the biggest reasons people live in bondage to past failures, or mistakes, or bad relationships, or lost opportunities is they do not forgive the people who have hurt them or held them back. Mary Johnson is not one of those people.

Mary had a twenty-year-old son named Laramiun Byrd. He got into a fight at a party with a sixteen-year-old boy named Oshea Israel, who shot and killed him. Laramiun was Mary's only son.

Oshea was tried, convicted, and sent to Stillwater Prison in Minnesota, with a sentence of twenty-five years. Mary wanted to meet Oshea face-to-face and ask him why he took her son's life, so more than eleven years later she sent a request for a meeting. Oshea said no. So Mary waited nine months and tried again. This time the murderer said yes, and when Mary arrived for the meeting, they began to talk. And talk. And talk. The meeting lasted two hours.

"I found out that your son's and my life paralleled," Oshea said later. "We had been through some of the same things, and somehow we got crossed. And I took his life—without even knowing him. But when I met you, he became human to me."[1]

After Mary left the meeting, she realized she'd just hugged her son's murderer. That's when she began to feel something strange. "I began to feel this movement in my feet. It moved up my legs and it just moved up my body. When I felt it leave me, I instantly knew that all that anger and hatred and animosity I had in my heart for you for twelve years was over. I had totally forgiven you."[2] And with that, Mary was able to move on with her life. Her son was still gone, but so was Mary's bitterness, releasing her to move forward.

The reason unforgiveness keeps people trapped in their past and unable to move forward is that it prevents them both from assessing their present appropriately and from seeing the future clearly. Think about it this way—if you want to drive from your house or apartment to the grocery store, you put your car into gear and step on the gas. To get to your destination safely, you must keep your eyes on the road in front of you. If you try to make the trip looking solely into the rearview mirror, you will crash.

The same principle applies to your life. If you keep looking backward at what happened, could or should have happened, or what did not happen, then you can't move forward. This is why so many people crash in life—because they won't forgive. The good things God has for your future are in front of you, not behind you. Unforgiveness blocks your capacity to see what's in front of you because it keeps you looking back.

Unforgiveness might be the most significant blockage or barrier to the breakthroughs God wants to bring to your life, to His church, and to our country. Honestly, I used to think this wasn't really a big deal. Plenty of us have unresolved situations or relationships, and we move on and seem to function just fine. But the Holy Spirit began to work on my own heart in the area of unforgiveness and revealed something shocking, something I had never noticed before. It has been in Scripture the entire time, but somehow I'd missed it. Mary Johnson had not missed it, but apparently I had. That is, until God revealed to me (although I should have seen it before) that He connects His forgiveness of us with our forgiveness of others. This was a tough pill for me to swallow, but it's there in the Bible. You can find it in the Lord's Prayer: "And forgive us our debts [trespasses] as we have also forgiven our debtors [those who trespass against us]."³ And that makes no sense either. But there it is.

You can find it again in verses 14 and 15 of Matthew 6, where Jesus explained, "If you forgive other people when they sin against you, your heavenly Father will also forgive you. But if you do not forgive others their sins, your Father will not forgive your sins."

*Gulp.* Both of these are pretty clear statements of how forgiveness works in God's world. Let's go back to the Lord's Prayer for a moment. Jesus prayed, "Forgive us our debts as we also have forgiven our debtors." Notice Jesus was not telling us to forgive the way God forgives, or the way God wants us to forgive. What He's really saying is, the way in which you forgive others is the standard that God will use to forgive you. It's an if-then proposition. *If* you forgive others, *then* God will forgive you.

This principle is not isolated to one scripture in one place in the Bible; it's communicated over and over again. Jesus said, "Whenever you stand praying, forgive, if you have anything against anyone, so that your Father who is in heaven will also forgive you your transgressions. But if you do not forgive, neither will your Father who is in heaven forgive your transgressions."⁴ Jesus was not saying that if we don't forgive someone, we are not going to heaven. The Word of God is clear on that—unforgiveness doesn't equal a lack of salvation or cancellation of the promise of eternal life. Forgiveness for eternal salvation was accomplished on the cross.

But you and I also need to practice forgiveness on a daily basis to maintain the intimacy of our relationship with God. That's the forgiveness Jesus is talking about. An unforgiving person living an unforgiving life means a life lived looking backward, robbed of peace, and greatly hindered in the ability to hear God's voice and have intimacy with Him. God is so serious about the importance of forgiveness that He links our willingness to forgive others with His daily forgiveness of us.

The world of the Amish, a peace-loving people who live isolated from modern conveniences and make faith the center of their lives, demonstrated forgiveness in 2006 when a thirty-two-year-old truck driver named Charles Roberts burst into an Amish schoolhouse and shot ten schoolgirls. Five died, then he turned the gun on himself. The horrific and senseless tragedy forced the eyes of the world onto the Amish, who like to go about their lives and remain hidden from the world. They don't like much attention. But their forgiveness of Charles Roberts, and his family, rocked the media.

The day of the mass murder, Amish people were already offering forgiveness. The grandfather of one of the girls came forward first, offering forgiveness to the killer that same afternoon. The demonstration of biblical forgiveness was shocking and controversial.

That same afternoon, an Amish contingent visited the family of Charles Roberts, offering condolences for their loss. Can you imagine visiting the family of someone who murdered your child, or your friend's child, and offering forgiveness the same day? It's beyond shocking; it's unfathomable. And you already know what I'm going to say, but it's true again. This kind of forgiveness does not make any sense.

But the offers of forgiveness continued. The Amish turned out in force to attend the funeral of Charles Roberts. And over and over, the Roberts family was told, "We are so sorry for your loss." They were overwhelmed with the compassion and care shown to them by the Amish community who had lost five children through the actions of their son. Through it all, they began to understand, and to see, that forgiveness is not a feeling, but a choice. And ultimately, they knew they had to forgive their son, although they'd never be able to understand why he had done it.

"I don't have to stop feeling anger, hurt, and utter bewilderment at the horrific decisions Charlie had made," his mother recently told a magazine writer. "I only had to make a choice: to forgive."[5]

Forgiving other people is what God expects us to do. One of Jesus' disciples named Peter once came up to Him and asked, "Lord, how often shall my brother sin against me, and I forgive him? Up to seven times?" Peter knew the religious leaders were only required to forgive someone twice, and if they really wanted to be gracious, to forgive someone three times. So Peter thought he was really doing something special when he asked about forgiving someone seven times, because that was double the rule, plus one!

But Jesus wasn't handing out gold stars to Peter that day. "I do not say to you, up to seven times, but up to seventy times seven," said Jesus. Then he told a story:

> The kingdom of heaven is like a certain king who wanted to settle accounts with his servants. And when he had begun to settle accounts, one was brought to him who owed him ten thousand talents [a form of money]. But as he was not able to pay, his master commanded that he be sold, with his wife and children and all he had, and that payment be made.
>
> The servant therefore fell down before him, saying, "Master, have patience with me, and I will pay you all."
>
> Then the master of that servant was moved with compassion, released him, and forgave him the debt.

What incredible, unbelievable forgiveness! Ten thousand talents was equal to fifteen thousand years worth of wages for the average person. In today's dollars, it is equivalent to $7.5 billion. That amount of money is almost beyond imagining, and it would be impossible to pay back. The servant, if he earned the usual salary for a working man of that day and age, would have needed 150,000 years to pay off the debt. There's no way. But that's not the end of the story, because the servant did something shocking next.

> That servant went out and found one of his fellow servants who owed him a hundred denarii; and he laid hands on him and took him by the throat, saying, "Pay me what you owe!"
>
> So his fellow servant fell down at his feet and begged him, saying, "Have patience with me, and I will pay you all."

This time the debt was much more doable. A hundred denarii is equivalent to roughly $17,000 in our current economy. The debt was comparable to a car loan; it might have taken a few years to pay it back, but it was doable.

The servant's answer should have been easy, right? He had been forgiven himself of a huge debt, so he should be feeling generous, when he compared the $7.5 billion to the relatively paltry $17,000. The servant who'd been forgiven by his master should then offer that same forgiveness to his fellow servant. But he didn't. Instead, he had him thrown into prison until he could pay the debt. Jesus was saying that what we have been forgiven is astronomical in comparison to the forgiveness we should offer others.

But there's still more. When the news got back to the master, he was not happy.

When his fellow servants saw what had been done, they were very grieved, and came and told their master all that had been done. Then his master, after he had called him, said to him, "You wicked servant! I forgave you all that debt because you begged me. Should you not also have had compassion on your fellow servant, just as I had pity on you?" And his master was angry, and delivered him to the torturers until he should pay all that was due to him.

Heavy stuff. Then Jesus wrapped up the story with this shocking statement: "So My heavenly Father also will do to you if each of you, from his heart, does not forgive his brother his trespasses."[6]

Is God so serious about people forgiving others that He will allow us to be tormented and tortured when we refuse to forgive? Jesus wasn't saying God will torture us. The wealthy ruler in the story did not torture the servant but turned him over to the tormenters who did. So Jesus was saying that God will simply withhold protection from us and give the enemy and his henchmen the legal authority to do the tormenting. And this is the way so many people are living their lives—tormented, tortured, and burdened.

The torture is not God's will for your life—freedom and Tree of Life living is. But He allows the torment to serve as a reminder, or a symptom, that something is deeply wrong in your life and needs to be addressed. Jesus was saying that unforgiveness is a sin God takes more seriously than perhaps anything else. Why? Because unforgiveness is a sign we have devalued God's forgiveness of us, like in the story where the servant devalued his master's forgiveness.

Unforgiveness of others reveals that our own hearts are not grateful for God's forgiveness of us. In essence, our refusal to forgive others dishonors the price Jesus paid on the cross. When we do not forgive, either ourselves or someone else, we are saying that Jesus' death may satisfy God, but it doesn't satisfy us.

One of the big reasons we live in torment and don't forgive is because we don't recognize the sins of unforgiveness in our own lives. The apostle Paul described some clear signs: "Let all bitterness and wrath and anger and clamor and slander be put away from you, along with all malice. Be kind to one another, tender-hearted, forgiving each other, just as God in Christ also has forgiven you."[7]

In your own heart, be careful to make yourself alert to signs of wrath, anger, clamor, slander, and malice. You could sum all these up as bitterness, meaning an irritable state of mind that keeps a person in perpetual animosity that inclines him or her to harsh and judgmental opinions of people and things. Bitterness affects how we look, what we say, and what we do. Here's how bitterness can manifest:

- *Wrath* means "burning rage." A wrathful person's disposition is loud and passionately explosive. Euphemisms for someone full of wrath include "He lost his cool" or "She lost her temper."
- *Anger* is quiet, simmering below the surface. It can be covered with a smile that doesn't seem sincere. You know the look—a smile on the mouth, but not the eyes.
- *Clamor* refers to an outcry, shouting, or screaming. Clamor is an unbridled use of the tongue to verbally tear down the character of someone else. Clamor is public verbal vengeance.
- *Slander* is profane and abusive speech.
- *Malice* is an outworking of evil, taking a bitter attitude and

bitter words and putting them into action against someone else.

Notice the progression? Bitterness affects a person's mood and disposition. If it's not addressed quickly, bitterness seeps into our conversations through snide remarks, sarcasm, and unhealthy comments. Finally, unresolved bitterness can result in unhealthy and damaging actions.

A woman named Pascale Kavanagh learned this lesson when she chose to forgive her mother. Pascale came from a dysfunctional childhood where her mother hit her, threw plates at her, and called her names. The treatment continued into adulthood, with her mother calling once a week to berate her about her friends, academics, and appearance. To save her sanity, Pascale moved across the country and distanced herself from the abuse. When Pascale had a daughter, her mother directed her rage at her granddaughter. Pascale wanted nothing more than to never hear from her mother again.

Then something strange happened. Pascale's mother suffered severe brain damage from a series of strokes and ended up in the hospital, without the ability to speak or understand speech. Pascale was the only relative available, so she felt she needed to help. She stayed by her mother's side reading and talking to her, but not knowing if she understood anything. Over a period of months, her anger diminished. One day, an exhausted Pascale suddenly laid her head down in her mother's lap. "And the hatred went away. It was just . . . gone. For the first time, I stopped condemning her. And that gave me peace."[8]

Pascale couldn't forget the way her mother had treated her or her daughter, but forgiveness didn't minimize the offense. It had happened and it was a big deal. What her mother had done was wrong.

Pascal's forgiveness was also not the same as reconciliation. When she forgave her mother and let go of what her mother had done to her, she wasn't able to reclaim and refashion the relationship into what it should have been. In some cases, reconciliation may not be the best choice. For a relationship to be restored, three things have to happen:

- Repentance (going in the right direction)
- Restitution (making things right)
- Rebuilding of trust (proving yourself through words and actions)

Since Pascale's mother was not capable of any of those things, a true reconciliation could not take place. But even if those three things can't or don't happen, forgiveness can still happen, benefiting the one who was wronged.

Forgiveness is also not forgetting what happened. "Forgive and forget" is misleading, because you may never forget what has happened to you. Pascale couldn't. But what God wants to do is bigger than that, because true forgiveness allows God to heal our hearts and remove the pain so that when you remember what happened to you, you also don't have to relive the pain that is associated with it.

Forgiveness is not easy, but when you choose to forgive, the feelings will follow. God will give you the strength and the way. "My grace is sufficient for you," He said. "My power is made perfect in weakness."[9] Don't ever measure your circumstances by your own ability. If you do, the act of forgiveness will seem impossible. But with God, it's not.

Here are the steps to forgiveness. Why don't you prayerfully follow these steps today and see what God is going to do?

1. Thank God for forgiving you.
2. Ask God, "Who do I need to forgive, and for what?"
3. Repent of your sin of unforgiveness.
4. Forgive each offense from your heart: "Lord, I choose to forgive _____ from my heart for _____. Lord, is there anything else I need to forgive him or her for? Before God, I declare _____ is no longer in my debt.
5. Seal it with a blessing (Luke 6:27–28; Romans 12:14).
6. Commit to choosing not to rehash or obsess on the offense.
7. Make "pre-forgiveness" a lifestyle. Remember that people are going to occasionally hurt or disappoint you. Be ready to forgive them as soon as it happens because if you don't, you open the door to be surprised. This heightens the possibility of your emotions taking over and leading you to get stuck in what they did to you, instead of quickly forgiving them. Pre-forgiveness simply means you have already made up your mind to forgive.

When Oshea Israel murdered her only son, Mary Johnson chose the path of forgiveness. But that's not the end of *her* story. After she met Oshea in prison, they became friends. When Oshea was released after serving seventeen years of his sentence, Mary put together a homecoming party. The two began to speak around the country and together tell their story of forgiveness.

Today, they live next door to each other and watch out for

each other. Oshea is like a son to her, the son he took from her with a gun. It's an astonishing story that shows forgiveness is possible and can bring life and hope where there was death and bitterness.

If forgiveness is indeed a choice, even if it makes no sense, please choose it. Today.

## POINTS TO REMEMBER

- One of the most inexplicable benefits of following God, and something that mostly defies logic, is God's forgiveness.
- One of the biggest reasons people live in bondage to past failures or mistakes, or bad relationships or lost opportunities is they do not forgive the people who have hurt them or held them back.
- Unforgiveness might be the most significant blockage or barrier to the breakthroughs God wants to bring to your life, to His church, and to our country.
- In the Lord's Prayer, Jesus prayed, "Forgive us our debts, as we also have forgiven our debtors." What Jesus was saying is the way in which you forgive others is the standard that God will use to forgive you. *If* you forgive others, *then* God will forgive you.
- We need to practice forgiveness on a daily basis to maintain the intimacy of our relationship with God.
- Be careful to make yourself alert to signs of wrath, anger, clamor, slander, and malice in your own life. These are signs of unforgiveness.
- Forgiveness is not easy, but when you choose to forgive, the feelings will follow. Forgiveness is a choice.

## QUESTIONS TO PONDER

1. Do you feel that God has forgiven you for your past mistakes? Does God's forgiveness make sense to you, or is it difficult to understand and grab hold of?

2. Because God has forgiven us, He expects us to do the same toward others. Is this a new concept for you? Are there people in your life, past or present, who need to be forgiven so you can move forward?

3. How can unforgiveness act like a barrier to positive change in your life? Is this something you'd like to act on today?

4. Have you ever noticed the part of the Lord's Prayer that talks about forgiving others before? Sometimes it's easy to memorize and repeat something but not internalize it.

5. What do you think about the challenge to practice forgiveness on a daily basis? If it deepens your relationship with God, are you willing to try it? What might be a first step for you?

6. Becoming aware of wrath and malice and bitterness in your life is an important practice that will help you become aware of unforgiveness. Is there an area of your life where you struggle with these feelings?

7. Who needs your forgiveness today?

# CHAPTER 19

# Love Found

*To cheat oneself out of love is the most terrible*
*deception; it is an eternal loss for which there is*
*no reparation, either in time or in eternity.*

—SØREN KIERKEGAARD

While Søren had formally ended his relationship with Regine and then dedicated himself heart and soul to his writing and study, he never really fell out of love with her. With all the love letters he wrote to her, the most powerful and poignant is the final letter he wrote to her—his last will and testament.

After the painful breakup, Regine had moved on and married her piano teacher, Herr Schlegel. Not long after that, Søren attempted to rekindle a friendship with Regine, but Herr Schlegel was against it, so nothing ever happened. Even though they lived in the same city, the lovers never met face-to-face again.

But in his final will, written in his own hand, Kierkegaard

showed the impact Regine had on his life in this, his last word on their passionate love affair.[1]

The letter was addressed to Søren's brother, Peter, and found locked inside Kierkegaard's desk to be opened after his death.

> Dear Brother,
>
> It is, of course, my will that my former fiancée, Mrs. Regine Schlegel [née Olsen], inherit without condition whatever little I may leave. If she herself will not accept it, she is to be asked if she would be willing to administer it for distribution to the poor.
>
> What I wish to give expression to is that to me an engagement was and is just as binding as a marriage, and that therefore my estate is her due, exactly as if I had been married to her.

Even though they had not married, Søren's heart was still bound to Regine's, and he considered her his first and only true love. He left her everything, exactly as if she was really his wife.

In addition to the will, inside Søren's desk was another sealed document. This second handwritten document was Søren's *literary* will and testament, regarding the legacy of words and ideas he left behind in his writings. In his books, papers, and stories, he had at times written about loving Regine without using her name, so in this note he called her the "unidentified one."

> The unidentified one whose name shall one day be identified—to whom all my activity as an author is dedicated—is my erstwhile fiancée, Mrs. Regine Schlegel.

Even though Søren had broken the engagement with Regine and had not spoken to her since the breakup, he still loved her with all his heart, and in this letter he formally dedicated every single thing he'd ever written to her. In essence, every one of Kierkegaard's words were written in her honor.

In his forty-two years of life, Søren wrote books, articles, papers, open letters, private letters, and more than seven thousand pages in his journals. The hundreds of thousands of words he wrote still endure and impact people today. Scholars, students, and readers of all kinds around the world read and meditate on his works.

Søren is now considered one of the great philosophers in human history, as well as a theologian, poet, and social critic. Scholars agree he was the first existentialist philosopher. Much of his work is revolutionary and deals with the concept of a faith-based love relationship between man and Jesus Christ. To Søren, faith was passion.

Yet all this work, the totality of his thoughts, ideas, and words, he dedicated to the first and only woman he ever loved, Regine. She was his inspiration, and though ultimately he couldn't be the husband she deserved, she carried his love.

Toward the end of his life, in a spirit of gratefulness he wrote this in a letter to her: "Thank you for everything I owe to you; thank you for the time you were mine . . . thank you my enchanting teacher, you lovely lily, you, my teacher . . . thank you for everything I have learned, if not from your wisdom, then from your lovely character; thank you also for your tears that have matured me so immensely."[2]

He also explained why he chose the path that he did when, with his writing gift, he surely could have chosen an easier path and gained riches and fame. "I have not been tempted by the honor and esteem of the world; I have belonged to something higher, gladly made sacrifices, gladly sought out dangers in order to have the honor of serving the oft-despised cause of truth; yet all my fame—that is our will—shall be owing to, shall belong to you, our own dear little Regine, you whose grace once enchanted and whose grief forever moved him whom neither the world's flattery nor its opposition has moved."[3]

In the end, the only thing that mattered to Søren was love, both the love of Regine and the love of God. Everything he said and everything he wrote flowed from this love. "Come out of this halfway condition," he wrote, in a challenge meant to wake up and stir the hearts of the churchgoers of his generation. "I am convinced that God is love," he cried out.

To a generation living in a "Christian country" and made up of churchgoing folk who thought of religion as a system of rules and laws, this was a powerful rallying cry from one of their own.

While Søren and Regine's brief but intense love relationship did not have a conventional "they lived happily ever after" ending, it did have a significant impact, creating a ripple effect on their families and friends, and the community around them. In the decades since Søren's untimely death, the ripple effect has reached far beyond his native country of Denmark and continued internationally through the fields of literature, theology, poetry, and philosophy.

Søren's message that God loves each of us personally not only resonated when he was alive, but it resonates still today. "God loves you" is a simple message, but it gets diluted and almost extinguished in the distractions of daily life and in a culture determined to find love in all the wrong places.

God loves each one of us, and that love lasts, even through rejection. Remember the cycle of love from the introduction?

# THE CYCLE OF LOVE

## *LOVE IS GIVEN—LOVE IS REJECTED—*
## *LOVE IS ACCEPTED*

You can see this cycle in Søren and Regine's story. On Regine's side, she freely gave her love to Søren, then was rejected by him when he broke up with her eleven months later, resulting in heartbreak and personal devastation. Later in life she learned that while their relationship had failed, and she ended up marrying another man, Søren still loved her and dedicated his life's work to her.

On Søren's side, he pledged his love to Regine both in person and in beautiful, fiery love letters. He asked her for her hand in marriage, then rejected her and went through the pain of a breakup caused by his own physical and emotional issues. Ultimately, he never married.

Later, he circled back around in his writing to acknowledge his love for her and the immense impact she had on his life and work. The failed relationship with Regine propelled him into a passionate love affair with God. And in the end, this epic love affair, and the cycle of love given-rejected-accepted, still impacts our world today through Kierkegaard's written words and thoughts.

As powerful as the love of these two human beings was, however, it's nothing, *nothing at all,* compared to the love God has for you. God is, like Søren, a suitor who wants your heart for His own. He loves and adores you and proclaims it in His love letter, a collection of sixty-six sacred, authentic, and historical books we call the Bible.

His love is proclaimed in writings made up of history, law, prophecy, poetry, love songs, stories, parables, Gospels, letters, and revelations. His passion shows in the beauty of earth, space, sky, and sea, created just for you. His desire for a relationship with you is mirrored in the relationships of human beings on display all around us, and all the emotions and turbulent passions therein. He knows what it's like to be rejected—He's been rejected every day in every way, in an unending repeat of the cycle of love with His people.

Yet.

God offers you His pure and unblemished love, in a relationship where He will do all the work, and all you have to do is accept His love. He only asks you for one thing—to make a choice.

Will you accept His love?

Will you choose to live loved?

There came a time when I had to make that choice. As long as I can remember, I wanted to be an attorney. Even as far back as kindergarten and first grade, I was a kid who loved to talk and reason and argue, and others saw that in me too. I'd been given the gift of argument and speech from the first moment I breathed oxygen into my lungs. As an older kid, I remember watching *L.A. Law* on television, and I felt deep inside that becoming an attorney and pursuing justice would be my mission in life. It felt good and it felt right.

But it wasn't right. The summer of my senior year in high school, I was working as a counselor at a Christian camp on the grounds of Montreat College in Montreat, North Carolina. I'd been going to that camp for years with my church youth group and that summer, I worked as a camp counselor and helped facilitate a youth conference for thousands of young people. It was exciting to go from attending to working and serving, and I began to have a glimmer that there might be something for me to do beyond a profession in the law.

One particular camp speaker made an impact on me when he talked about discovering God's calling, and I went up to him one evening after the service and on impulse, blurted out, "I think God is calling me to ministry full time. I used to think a calling would come like a blinding light, a Saul-on-the-road-to-Damascus kind of thing. So maybe I'm misled or dreaming this up, but this is what I think."

I'll never forget his response. I still think about it every day of my life. "The calling is not just a moment," he said. "It's something you have to answer every day of your life."

What the speaker was saying to me is that I had to make a choice. To pursue the law and become an attorney was the desire of my heart from the time I was a small child, but I was feeling a calling to enter full-time ministry. And I was going to have to make a choice between the two. The speaker's response forced me to wrestle with this decision and led me to realize I had come to a crossroads, a place where I had to decide what I was going to do and if I was going to commit my life to answer the call I was feeling inside my soul.

Would I choose God's way or my way?

Come to think of it, this *was* like a road-to-Damascus moment. The call had been made clear to me, and I had to make a choice. Listen to the call, or continue on my same path?

Once I was in college and beginning to lean into my ministry studies, I felt the tug again. I wondered at times, *Did I make the right choice? Will I be able to make it in the ministry, or would I do better as an attorney? Will I be able to support myself and provide for a family? Will I be able to grow into this role and this calling? Will God use me? Will people listen to me?* And ultimately, the big question: *Will whatever I end up doing in ministry make a difference in this world?*

But what was interesting is that whenever I began to struggle with this idea of calling, God would open an amazing door. Favor would come in. My calling would be reinforced. And each time, I learned to love and trust God on a deeper level. One of my college professors who taught Greek saw something in me and recommended me for an educational program in Italy.

Somehow I was chosen and flew off to Rome to join the program and ultimately meet with Pope John Paul II. There, I happened to meet a woman who was impressed with my contribution to the group. She sat on the board of the World Council of Churches, and she recommended me for a program in Germany, so off I went to Germany. All this for a kid who, prior to those experiences, had never been out of the United States.

Because I was choosing to follow God's calling, He whisked me away on an adventure that I could have never imagined. God wouldn't allow me to doubt my calling because I was too busy walking through door after door, all of them opened by God as He led me deeper into ministry and a love relationship with Him.

This path hasn't been all roses and candlelight though. There are struggles and doubts and missteps along the way. It's not always easy and it certainly isn't always clear. But when you become aware of God's love, and that this incredible love is directed at you personally, it becomes a game changer.

Reading God's love letter over and over, and soaking in His love for you, is the most powerful and life-changing experience you will ever have. And at some point understanding His love means you will have to make a choice. Are you going to accept it and live loved? Or are you going to reject it?

Each person's path to a relationship with God is different, because you and your story are unique. You're still writing your story. So you might have accepted God's love as a child, but you've moved on from that first love experience and the relationship has dwindled away. Or you might have made a decision to follow God as a teenager or young adult, but life happened, and in the midst of the struggle and hurt and disappointments life can bring, you forgot how much God loves you and wants to be part of your life.

Maybe life has knocked you down and beaten you up, and God's love feels distant, or even nonexistent. Or perhaps you've never really known or experienced God's love in the first place, so this is all new to you. God might have, to you, been a set of rules and laws that you tried to keep, but couldn't (because in the end, none of us can) and so you gave up, feeling like God was an old man somewhere in the sky keeping tabs on your mistakes and getting ready to issue a report card on your failures.

Each person's path is different, but God is the same. He loves you, He wants you, and His mission is to make sure you know how much He loves you. He's always there, He's always waiting, and He's always ready to meet you on that prodigal road with a ring and a robe.

God loves you.

Will you love Him back?

If you do, all the treasures He offers are yours. "The kingdom of heaven is like a treasure hidden," wrote Matthew in his gospel.[4] I urge you, choose the treasure.

"For life is more than food, and the body more than clothes," wrote Luke in his gospel.[5] *Choose the more.*

"If you return to the Almighty, you will be restored," says the book of Job.[6] *Choose restoration.*

"We have this treasure in earthen vessels, so that the surpassing greatness of the power will be of God, and not from ourselves," wrote Paul in 2 Corinthians.[7] *Choose the power of God.*

"Instruct those who are rich in this present world not to be conceited or to fix their hope on the uncertainty of riches, but on God, who richly supplies us with all things to enjoy," wrote Paul to Timothy.[8] *Choose God's riches.*

"Because they are united in love, I pray that their hearts may be encouraged by all the riches that come from a complete understanding of the full knowledge of the Messiah, who is the mystery of God," wrote Paul to the Colossian church.[9] *Choose the knowledge of the Messiah.*

"No one can serve two masters; for either he will hate the one and love the other, or he will be devoted to one and despise the other," wrote Matthew.[10] *Choose your master.*

"And I am convinced that nothing can ever separate us from God's love. Neither death nor life, neither angels nor demons, neither our fears for today nor our worries about tomorrow—not even the powers of hell can separate us from God's love. No power in the sky above or in the earth below—indeed, nothing in all creation will ever be able to separate us from the love of God that is revealed in Christ Jesus our Lord," wrote Paul in Romans.[11] *Choose love.*

Cling to God, and let His love radically change your life with the riches only He can bring. He's madly in love with you, you know.

# Acknowledgments

Susy Flory: It was so great to work with you! Thank you for your wisdom and skill.

Mel Berger: Thank you for believing in me and fighting for me.

The Thomas Nelson Team: Brian Hampton, Webster Younce, Janene MacIvor, Aryn VanDyke, and Sara Broun: It has been such an honor to work with you! Thank you for your commitment to producing great content that inspires the world.

My Dream Team: Chris Roslan, Scott Spiewak, Martijn van Tilborgh, Gregory Mitchell, Raoul Davis, Art Franklin, Sly King, Tijuanna Williams, and Lamonte Austin: I remain grateful for your belief in this book and your work on this project.

To my TWC & MIBF Family: Thank you for your continued prayer, support, and encouragement.

To Ty, Eden, and Ethan: I love you more than words can say! Thank you for sharing me.

# Notes

## Prologue

1. Søren Kierkegaard, *Kierkegaard's Writings, Volume 25: Letters and Documents* (Princeton: Princeton University Press, 2009), 63, 67.

## Introduction

1. Tim Worstall, "Steve Jobs and the Don't Settle Speech," Forbes.com, October 8, 2011, https://www.forbes.com/sites/timworstall/2011/10/08/steve-jobs-and-the-dont-settle-speech/#76a0e1237437.
2. "A Genius Departs," *Economist,* October 8, 2011, http://www.economist.com/node/21531530.
3. "Steve Jobs Quotes: The Man in His Own Words," The Guardian, October 6, 2011, https://www.theguardian.com/technology/2011/oct/06/steve-jobs-quotes.
4. Matthew 22:37–40.

## Chapter 1: Signed, Sealed, Delivered, I'm Yours

1. Kierkegaard, *Kierkegaard's Writings,* 73.
2. Søren Kierkegaard, *Papers and Journals: A Selection* (New York: Penguin, 1996), 101
3. Kierkegaard, *Kierkegaard's Writings,* 73.
4. Genesis 9:12–17.

## Chapter 2: C'mon . . . Just Believe!

1. Abraham's original name was Abram, but at one point God changed his name to Abraham. To avoid any confusion, I'll be calling him Abraham all the way through.
2. Genesis 12:1–3.
3. Genesis 15:1–6 NLT.
4. Hebrews 6:17.
5. Genesis 17:5–8, 15–16 NLT.
6. Genesis 17:10–14.

## Chapter 3: Achy Breaky Heart

1. Exodus 19:3–6 NLT.
2. Exodus 20:18–19 NLT.
3. Exodus 32:15.

## Chapter 4: Ugh! More Rules. Really?!

1. Psalm 42:1–2.
2. Psalm 63:1–8.

## Chapter 5: I Love You . . . This Much

1. Søren Kierkegaard, *Works of Love* (New York: Harper and Row, 1962), i.
2. Matthew 1:1 ESV.
3. Martin H. Manser, *The Westminster Collection of Christian Quotations*, (Louisville: Westminster John Knox Press, 2001), 177.

## Chapter 6

1. Exodus 3:13–15 ESV.
2. Ira Berkow, "Baseball; A Most Extraordinary Fella," *New York Times*, December 25, 1992, http://www.nytimes.com/1992/12/25 /sports/baseball-a-most-extraordinary-fella.html.
3. Kristen Noel, "Interview: Kris Carr, Crazy Sexy Awakening," Best Self Magazine, May 18, 2015, https://bestselfmedia.com /interview-kris-carr/.

4. Ibid.

5. Elizabeth Castoria, "Interview with Kris Carr," Veg News, February 8, 2009, http://vegnews.com/articles/page .do?pageId=336&catId=5.

6. Joel 3:10 NKJV.

7. Libby Copeland, "Who Was She?" *Washington Post*, July 27, 2017, https://www.washingtonpost.com/graphics/2017/lifestyle /she-thought-she-was-irish-until-a-dna-test-opened-a-100-year-old -mystery/?utm_term=.3cbf036716ed.

8. 1 John 4:4.

9. John 11:21–27.

## Chapter 7: The Good Shepherd

1. Stephanie McNeal, "These Parents Changed Their Baby's Unusual Name When She Was 3 Months Old," Buzzfeed News, August 11, 2016, https://www.buzzfeed.com/stephaniemcneal/these-parents -changed-their-daughters-name-when-she-was-3-mo?utm_term= .jujRplDbX#.uyOdlrZm3.

2. Psalm 23 NKJV.

3. Genesis 48:15.

4. John 10:11.

5. John 10:9.

## Chapter 8: The Fixer

1. "Lost: How a Dead Man Saved Two Dallas Hikers," D Magazine, December 2006, https://www.dmagazine.com /publications/d-magazine/2006/december/lost/.

2. Exodus 15:25–27 NKJV.

3. Matthew 6:25–27.

## Chapter 9: Father God (Not the Godfather)

1. Luke 15:1.

2. James 1:15 CEV.

3. John 10:10.

4. Luke 15:17–20 THE MESSAGE.

5. Luke 15:26–32.

## Chapter 10: More Than Enough

1. Juju Chang and Cathy Becker, "She Can't Stop Eating: Living with Prader-Willi Syndrome a Daily Struggle," ABC News, August 17, 2009, http://abcnews.go.com/GMA/story?id=8222023.

2. John 4:7–15 THE MESSAGE.

3. Jeremiah 2:13.

4. John 4:25–26 THE MESSAGE.

## Chapter 11: Simple

1. Avital Andrews, "Jacob Barnett's Curious and Computational Mind," *Pacific Standard*, May 19, 2017, https://psmag.com /magazine/jacob-barnett-30-under-30.

2. Acts 16:16–34.

3. Romans: 10:9.

4. Scott Parazynski, *The Sky Below* (Seattle: Little A, 2017), 171.

5. Genesis 15:5.

6. 1 John 4:19.

7. Romans 5:6, 8.

8. John 15:12.

9. John 13:35.

10. John 13:12–15, 17.

11. Arthur Boers, "What Henri Nouwen Found at Daybreak," *Christianity Today*, October 3, 1994, http://www.christianitytoday .com/ct/1994/october3/4tb028.html.

## Chapter 12: No Mountain High Enough

1. Kilian Jornet, "Training: Five Tips for Training and Competing in the Mountains," KilianJornet.cat accessed December 7, 2017, http://www.kilianjornet.cat/en/training/.

2. Luke 10:25–26, emphasis added.

3. Luke 10:30 NKJV.

4. Luke 10:31.

5. Myron Medcalf, "Purdue's Caleb Swanigan Has Changed His Body and His Life," ESPN, March 18, 2017, http://www.espn.com/mens-college-basketball/story/_/id/18523734/purdue-caleb-swanigan-overcoming-obesity-homelessness-become-big-nba-prospect.

6. Luke 10:33–35.

7. Luke 10:36–37.

## Chapter 13: Reliable GPS

1. John 14:1–4.

2. John 14:5–6.

3. Hebrews 9:22.

4. Genesis 4:3–5.

5. Genesis 22:2, 6–8, 11–14.

6. Exodus 12:3, 5, 7, 12–13.

7. 2 Corinthians 5:18–21 TLB.

8. John 1:29.

## Chapter 14: The Gift of Freedom, Part 1

1. Philip Sherwell, "2004 Tsunami: Petra Nemcova, the Supermodel Who Survived the Boxing Day Tragedy," *Telegraph*, December 26, 2014, http://www.telegraph.co.uk/news/worldnews/asia/thailand/11303121/2004-Tsunami-Petra-Nemcova-the-supermodel-who-survived-the-Boxing-Day-tragedy.html.

2. Genesis 2:16–17 NLT.

3. Genesis 2:23 NLT.

4. Genesis 3:1–13 NLT.

## Chapter 15: The Gift of Freedom, Part 2

1. Jacoba Urist, "What the Marshmallow Test Really Teaches About Self-Control," *Atlantic*, September 24, 2014, https://www.theatlantic.com/health/archive/2014/09/what-the-marshmallow-test-really-teaches-about-self-control/380673/.

2. James 1:14–15 NLT.

3. Romans 5:8.

4. John 14:15.

5. John 20:15–16 NKJV.

6. Matthew 5:17.

7. Deuteronomy 30:19–20.

## Chapter 16: The Gift of Hope

1. Joe Rudemiller, "From Enslavement to Enlightenment," *UC Magazine*, April 2012, http://magazine.uc.edu/issues/0412/cadet.html.

2. Jean-Robert Cadet, *Restavec: From Haitian Slave Child to Middle-Class American* (Austin, University of Texas Press, 1998).

3. Rudemiller, "From Enslavement to Enlightenment."

4. Ruth 1:1–18 NLT.

5. Matthew 5:6.

6. Ruth 2:2–3 NLT.

7. Ruth 2:8–12 NLT.

8. Ruth 4:11–15 NLT.

## Chapter 17: The Gift of Favor

1. Jennifer Earl, "Strangers Bring Waitress to Tears with $400 Tip, Then Even Bigger Surprise," *CBS News*, April 13, 2017, https://www.cbsnews.com/news/cayla-chandara-hawaii-waitress-huge-tip/.

2. Luke 1:45 NLT.

3. Luke 1:46–48 NLT.

4. Luke 1:34 NLT.

5. Luke 1:38 NASB.

6. Isaiah 54:2–3.

## Chapter 18: The Gift of Forgiveness

1. Dave Isay, "You Killed My Son . . . and I Forgive You," *Daily Beast*, October 23, 2013, http://www.thedailybeast.com/you-killed-my-sonand-i-forgive-you.

2. Ibid.

3. Matthew 6:12.

4. Mark 11:25–26 NASB.

5. Terri Roberts, "My Son Shot 10 Amish Girls in a Pennsylvania Schoolhouse," *Woman's Day*, February 19, 2016, http://www.womansday.com/life/inspirational-stories/a53626/terri-roberts-forgiven-excerpt/.

6. Matthew 18:21–35 NKJV.

7. Ephesians 4:31–32 NASB.

8. Brian Ayling, "3 True Stories of Forgiveness: I Forgave My Mother for Abusing Me," *Real Simple*, accessed December 9, 2017, https://www.realsimple.com/work-life/life-strategies/inspiration-motivation/stories-forgiveness#abusive-mother.

9. 2 Corinthians 12:9.

## Chapter 19: Love Found

1. D. Anthony Storm, "Other Posthumous Works: Letters and Documents," D. Anthony Storm's Commentary on Kierkegaard, accessed December 9, 2017, http://sørenkierkegaard.org/kierkegaard-letters-documents.html.

2. Søren Kierkegaard, *Kierkegaard's Writings, Volume 25: Letters and Documents* (Princeton: Princeton University Press, 2009), 323.

3. Ibid., 324.

4. Matthew 13:44.

5. Luke 12:23.

6. Job 22:23.

7. 2 Corinthians 4:7 NASB.

8. 1 Timothy 6:17 NASB.

9. Colossians 2:2 ISV.

10. Matthew 6:24 NASB.

11. Romans 8:38–39 NLT.

# About the Authors

Van Moody has a passion for transforming people, organizations, and the world. With a background in leadership, business, and ministry, he is qualified uniquely to position and empower people for health and success in every aspect of their lives.

Moody's compelling voice has been heard around the world and on various stages, including TEDx Birmingham, the 30th Anniversary of the March on Washington, with Pope John Paul II and his Pontifical Council in Rome, in Tokyo as an associate trainer for Dr. John Maxwell's EQUIP leadership organization, in Melbourne for Planet Shakers and as a keynote speaker for Bishop T. D. Jakes's Woman Thou Art Loosed Conference.

In 2016 Moody became a member of Dr. Oz's Core Team and has been featured several times on the *Dr. Oz Show* on ABC. He writes frequently for the *Christian Post* and Fox News and his articles also have been featured in *Essence Magazine, Investors' Business Daily, Forbes, American Express Open Forum, Maxim,* and many others.

He is the creator of The Advance Leadership Institute & Intensive that trains leaders globally. Moody also assists in leading

Macedonia International Bible Fellowship (MIBF), a global network of pastors and churches.

The Atlanta, Georgia, native is a graduate of DePauw University (Greencastle, Ind.), the Interdenominational Theological Center (Atlanta), Harvard University's Summer Leadership Institute (Cambridge, Mass.), and Oxford University (Oxford, England). He is currently pursuing his second doctoral degree at Biola University (La Mirada, CA).

In March 2006, Moody established The Worship Center in Birmingham. This thriving multisite church serves more than five thousand members, with five weekly services and an online campus viewed from as far away as Kuwait.

Moody lives in Birmingham, Alabama with his wife, Dr. Ty, their two children—Eden Sydney and Ethan Isaiah—and their golden-doodle dog, Teddy Bear.

For more info visit: vanmoody.org

Susy Flory is the *New York Times* bestselling author or coauthor of more than a dozen books. She lives in California and directs the West Coast Christian Writers Conference.

# OTHER BOOKS BY
# VAN MOODY

The right relationship will launch you to the heights of achievement; the wrong one will tether you to mediocrity. Your relationships will be your source of greatest joy and your venues of greatest pain. You need to evaluate your relationships intelligently. *The People Factor* shows you how, providing the tools to become stronger, happier, and healthier in all your relationships.

ISBN: 9781400205028

One question lies behind every struggle we face: How do I deal with myself? Behind all our stumbles, behind each of our missteps, behind every one of our failings lies an inability to handle what Van Moody calls the "I-factor." More than self-worth or self-respect, beyond even character and perception of purpose, the I-factor is about managing yourself—your whole life—well. In his inspiring book, *The I-Factor*, Moody reveals how to get hold of your I-factor.

ISBN: 9780718077587

VanMoody.org